ANNA TERESA CALLEN'S
MENUS
FOR
PASTA

Also by Anna Teresa Callen
The Wonderful World of Pizzas, Quiches, and Savory Pies

ANNA TERESA CALLEN'S
MENUS
FOR
PASTA

Drawings by Jennifer Geiger

Crown Publishers, Inc.   New York

Grateful acknowledgment is made for permission to use the following recipes:

"Cassata alla Sulmonese," Copyright © 1981 The New York Times Company. Reprinted by permission. "Fusilli alla Franca Falcone," Copyright © 1984 The New York Times Company. Reprinted by permission.

"Maccheroni alla Chitarra coi Funghi," "Lasagna in Brodo alla Lancianese," and "Parrozzo di Papa," Copyright © 1985 *Gourmet Magazine*. "Pasta con la Salsa Cruda," Copyright © 1981 *The New York Post*. "Sugo alla Bolognese," "Cavatelli con l'Arugola," Copyright © 1982 *The Daily News*.

"Crostata di Crema Jolanda," "Zucchine a Scapece," and "Granita di Caffè." Originally published in *Great Meals in Minutes*. Courtesy of Time-Life Books, Inc.

"Spaghetti Primavera," compliments of Sirio Maccione of Le Cirque Restaurant, New York City; "Troccoli alla Daunia," compliments of Ristorante Ciccolella of Foggia, Apulia, Italy; "Insalata Tricolore," compliments of Fulvio Tramontina, owner of Salta in Bocca Restaurant, New York City; "Tagliatelle alla Caprese," compliments of Gianni Minale, owner of Alfredo on the Park Restaurant, New York City.

"Ciambotta alla Federico Spera," compliments of Federico Spera; "Pere alla Gabriella," compliments of Gabriella Pace; "Spaghetti alla Puttanesca Lia Saraceni," compliments of Lia Saraceni; "Crema di Frutta Ermione," compliments of Hermie Kranzdorf.

"Funghi Farciti al Prosciutto Cotto e Salame" and "Tagliolini al Quattro Formaggi," inspired by Alfredo Viazzi, owner of Trattoria da Alfredo, New York City.

"Sorbetto di Mortelle e Ananas," adapted from a dessert by Bert Greene.

Published by Crown Publishers, Inc., One Park Avenue, New York, New York 10016, and simultaneously in Canada by General Publishing Company Limited

Manufactured in the United States of America

CROWN is a trademark of Crown Publishers, Inc.

Library of Congress Cataloging in Publication Data

Callen, Anna Teresa.
Anna Teresa Callen's menus for pasta.

1. Cookery (Macaroni) 2. Menus. I. Title.
TX809.M17C335 1984   641.8'22   84-23065
ISBN 0-517-55400-3

Design by Rhea Braunstein

10 9 8 7 6 5 4 3 2 1
First Edition

To my mother, Raffaella Vita-Colonna, a good cook who
didn't like to cook.

To my father, Giuseppe Vita-Colonna, a *buongustaio*
whose greatest hobby was to cook.

To my twin brother, Mimmo, who is lucky to have an
excellent cook for a wife.

To my husband, Harold, who enters the kitchen to boil
two eggs, but can enjoy with open spirit and mouth the
good food coming his way.

Last but not least to my two cats, Ivan, who will bite
anything coming from my fingers without a thought or
a sniff, and his sister, Mary Jane, who has to think five
times before accepting a morsel which does not come
from a can.

Contents

Acknowledgments, ix
Introduction, xi

The Basics
About Pasta, 3
Basic Recipes for Homemade Pasta, 7
Glossary of Pasta, 15
Tools and Utensils, 23
Ingredients, 27
Some Helpful Hints, 33
Basic Sauces, 35

The Menus
Preface to Menus, 45
Menus for Spring, 47
Menus for Summer, 52
Menus for Autumn, 57
Menus for Winter, 62

The Recipes
Appetizers, 71
Pastas, 109
Salads, 163
Desserts, 183

Index, 217

Acknowledgments

This book could not have been accomplished without the enthusiastic response of my faithful pupils in testing these recipes. I thank them all with gratitude. I am especially indebted for the support and devotion of the following students: Anna Marra, Roberto Talignani, Olga Aparicio, Martha Wolford, Herb Field, Susan Kotof, Martin Stain O'Hara, Charles Pinto, Irma Hyams, Linda Schieber, Susan Goldstein, Edith Manfredi Zoppi, Chuck and Felicia Berg, Mary Towner, Stephen Davis, Rose Friedlieb, Faith Bandklayder, and Louis and Tom Galterio.

Introduction

Many books have been written about pasta, but not one has treated pasta as the main dish to be served with an appetizer, a salad, and a dessert. This book does just that.

When I first came to this country, I was astounded by some of the meals I was served at dinner parties. The menus frequently consisted of spaghetti and salad, followed by a splashy dessert of garnished ice cream. The spaghetti sauce was all too often a runny mess and the salad made of raw, wilted spinach. *"Mamma mia!"* I would say to myself. *"This* is how they eat in America?"

In Italy, pasta is almost always a first course, or *I Primi.* Spaghetti is fine as family fare but is not considered good enough for guests, who warrant something more special. And spinach is hidden away in a stuffing or, if one *really* likes it, is delicately cooked in butter.

For years I sneered. Eventually, I learned to like raw spinach and "discovered" the Sicilian way of preparing it. At first, when I gave dinner parties, I served small portions of homemade pasta in order to leave room for the rest of the meal. If I used commercial pasta, I concocted elaborate *timballi* with special sauces. It was fifteen years before I realized that I could indeed serve pasta as a main course and not be ashamed of it. And it came about in this way:

I had been working for the Encyclopaedia Britannica in New York and had reached the coveted position of acting director of the International Editorial Department, a glory, alas, that lasted only three short months, because the established director of the Britannica decided to move the editorial offices to Chicago.

This left me with three choices: (1) move to Chicago, (2) go to Italy to finish the Italian version of the encyclopedia, (3) unemployment. I took the second choice.

When I returned six months later, I joined the ranks of the unemployed. Then one day a phone call started me on a new career. My ex-assistant, a bright young woman with whom I had become friendly, was working for a firm that was packaging a Time-Life book series. She knew how I loved to cook and had often eaten and praised my meals. "Anna Teresa," she started off, "how would you like to write some food articles for the series 'Family Creative Workshop'?" "How would I like to write some food articles?" I screeched with joy. "I'd love it." She went on to say that they were working on Volume 12, letter *P*. Could I write something about food starting with *p*? "Of course," I said without a moment's thought, *"pasta!"*

Writing the article was, to mix my metaphors, a piece of cake. Then came the tricky part: I had to cook all of the dishes I had mentioned for the photographic session. Naturally, I invited all my friends to eat the "props." The photographer was a gourmet and obligingly worked around me to keep the dishes hot so that he and my guests could enjoy the pasta at its best. A good deal of discussion followed the eating of my homemade cannelloni, ravioli, tortellini, *tagliatelle, maccheroni alla chitarra.* Which of the homemade pasta dishes was the best? No one could agree; they declared them all excellent. But the unanimous winner of the commercial pasta dishes was Timballo di Maccheroni alla Nonnina. Runner-up was Franca Falcone's Fusilli, a recipe my cousin Franca had wheedled out of the fishermen of Sorrento. All I can say is that everyone was in a state of euphoria. However, amid the signs of contentment I detected a few rumbles of discontent. When pressed they finally said, "Anna Teresa, your usual dinners tease us with your small portions of pasta. Give us a *pasta* dinner. We guarantee we'll eat all the pasta you can make."

"What a revelation! And to think that all this time I could have been giving you *nozze coi fichi secchi,*" I commented. "What's that?" they asked. "That," I answered, "is a good old Abruzzese saying that literally means 'serving at a wedding only dried figs.' Figuratively, it means 'feeding people cheaply.' " It hit me then that I had been treating my friends like guests instead of friends—an error I soon corrected. Before long, my friends had dubbed me the Pasta Maven of New York, a title I relish.

My aim in this book is to give appetizing (and for the most part, economical), easy-to-assemble menus that guide you toward making pasta into a delicious and sumptuous meal. In other words, to make *nozze coi fichi secchi*.

THE
BASICS

About Pasta

Whenever I start a new pasta course in my cooking school, I am invariably amazed to discover how many people still do not know the basics of cooking, making, and dressing pasta. No matter how many times the difference between factory-made, packaged dry pasta and the homemade type is explained, people will still say to me with a look of knowledge and envy in their eyes, "Of course, you make your own pasta!"—as though the only pasta worth eating is the one you make yourself.

Yes, I do make pasta at home, but I would never dream of making spaghetti, ziti, *penne*, rigatoni, fusilli, elbow macaroni, or bow ties; in short, none of the types of pasta one can buy packaged and well made by a pasta factory. I would never be able to reach their lightness, smoothness, compactness, their perfection. Why? Because this pasta is made with durum wheat or semolina and only a factory has the kind of machine able to break and appropriately knead those hard granular types of flours.

I am also a little bit suspicious of these pasta machines which, in seconds, start to spit out all sorts of pasta, just after the ingredients have been added and too little kneading has occurred. Homemade pasta needs at least twenty minutes of kneading and thirty minutes of rest before being processed.

For homemade pasta, only regular all-purpose, unbleached flour and eggs are used and the pasta is always flat or stuffed.

There are some homemade pastas made from semolina combined with flour (a good example are *orecchiette di Puglia* whose origins go back to Roman times), but like the whole-wheat pastas, *bigoli alla Veneta* or *pizzoccheri della Valtellina*, made with buckwheat flour, they belong to the regional recipes of the *cucina povera*, the cooking of the poor, mainly from the south. They provide a gamut of delightful rustic dishes for which the Italian cuisine is justly famous.

It happens that people read on the package of store-bought pasta "made with durum wheat or semolina," and off they go to buy durum flour and semolina—which, by the way, is durum flour before being milled. As I said, to knead this mixture properly, one needs a factory machine. If done at home, the result will be unsatisfactory, producing a pasty, doughy product—a long way from the *tagliatelle* or fettuccine noodles made with all-purpose flour with a texture that is tender and delicate but consistent when properly cooked.

Homemade pasta is the pasta of our ancestors; it has been made for centuries. And when I say our, I include all ancestors, because the noodle, which is the basic homemade shaped pasta, is indigenous to many civilizations. Which mother or grandmother didn't make *tagliatelle*, lokshen, lo mein, or whatever? In fact, the Orientals are the only ones using flours other than wheat flour, the staple of the Western world. The noodle is made with regular flour, preferably unbleached, and eggs. It can be broad or narrow; in Italian, it can be called *tagliolini*, *tagliatelle*, fettuccine, or *fettuccelle*. With the same noodle dough one makes lasagna strips (the best lasagna is indeed the homemade type), tortellini, ravioli, cannelloni, *pappardelle*, and others. These are the elegant, delicate pastas usually dressed with a rich sauce and reserved for special occasions; they are not as light as a simple dish of spaghetti dressed with a marinara sauce or fusilli with a basil and tomato sauce. On the whole, commercial pastas are infinitely more digestible and less fattening. Homemade pasta and factory-made pasta are two different birds, like a pheasant and a chicken. Would you want to eat a pheasant every day?

In these days of rushing all the time, a hand-cranked pasta machine that stretches and cuts the dough is a great help. Dough made with a food processor is excellent, provided you knead the dough by hand for at least ten or fifteen minutes after processing it. Although my mother doesn't approve, I kiss my food processor every time I use it! What a useful machine!

Ideally, homemade pasta should be eaten the day it is made.

However, if left to dry, it can be stored in a cool place or refrigerated for several weeks. It can also be frozen. Do not defrost before cooking. Gnocchi, ravioli, and tortellini freeze quite well, but they should be spread out on trays until frozen and bagged when hard. If you bag them while still fresh, they will lump together.

Another type of pasta that has become the rage of the entire country is the so-called fresh pasta. It is sold in many pasta and gourmet shops as well as in some supermarkets. In its own way, it is acceptable. The stuffed varieties, such as tortellini and ravioli, are rather good, but again this pasta should not be confused with true homemade pasta. These "fresh pastas" are made with durum wheat or semolina, with eggs sometimes added. The combination produces a smooth, durable pasta that can withstand time and handling. Homemade pasta, on the other hand, is more tender and delicate, and it breaks easily when dry. The texture of fresh pasta is often chewy and pasty, and for my taste, I much prefer a good factory-made pasta. However, when I want stuffed pasta shapes, I sometimes choose fresh pasta for its convenience, since these types are time-consuming to make by hand.

Many people believe that pasta is fattening. Not so; it is what you put on top that makes a dish of pasta fattening. If you go to Italy, you will seldom see as grossly fat people as you do in the United States. Italians do not have an obesity problem because they eat pasta, which expands the stomach and satisfies the appetite.

Pasta per se is an economical food and quite nutritious. It contains vitamins, especially E, and a fair amount of protein. The embryo of the wheat, a perfect food, is retained in properly processed factory-made pasta. This type of pasta contains many elements necessary to health and well-being—amino acids and minerals, especially phosphorus, which is beneficial to the brain.

A word about the origins of pasta: My first book, *The Wonderful World of Pizzas, Quiches, and Savory Pies*, begins with a quotation from the Bible in which Elijah eats a "cake" baked on a stone. In my opinion, that cake was the first pizza. That pizza, cut into strips and boiled in water or broth, became *tagliatelle* or noodles. It is true that China and Japan have a history of noodle making that goes back to 3000 B.C., but it is also true that Marco Polo, the Venetian traveler, didn't bring spaghetti to Italy in the thirteenth century; the history of our pasta making is also very ancient.

Without going back too far, let's start with the Etruscans, who lived in Italy during the fifth and fourth centuries B.C. The Etruscans were great artists and inventors, originators of the shovel and many other familiar domestic tools. It was this people who taught the Romans how to build an arch, unknown even to the Greeks. In one of their tombs, the Tomba dei Rilievi, in Cerveteri, two pillars dating from the fourth century B.C. still stand, hung with all the accouterments to make pasta—the wooden board, the rolling pin, the fluted cutting wheel—just like the ones used today in Romagna, Lazio, Abruzzo, and other regions of Italy.

Cicero (106–43 B.C.), the Roman orator, statesman, and philosopher, seems to have been quite greedy for *laganum*, the Latin name for lasagna. He loved to eat thin strips of pasta made with flour and water, cooked in a fat broth, and dressed with cheese, pepper, saffron, and cinnamon. Horace (65–8 B.C.), the Roman poet, loved pasta too. In one of his satires, after feeling sorry for the praetor Tiberio for not being able to go out without his five servants, he tells him how lucky is he who, being unimportant, can go anywhere alone, to the market and ask without shame the cost of the salad and the wheat, to the circus and the forum and finally home, undisturbed, to his "bowl of leeks, chick-peas and lasagna."

As for Marco Polo, he says in his book how he found in "those extreme lands" of Asia foods "similar to those we make [at home]" with wheat flour, and he calls them *"laganum."* In my opinion, Marco Polo had eaten quite a few bowls of lasagne well topped with cheese many times before his voyage to China in 1215.

An interesting piece of information is found in an Arab book, *Kitab Rugiar*, the Book of Roger, in which one reads that in the town of Trabia near Palermo, Sicily, a special food made with flour looked like threads and was known by the Arab word *itriyah*. In Sicily today, a kind of vermicelli called *trii* is still eaten. Roger II, king of Sicily, who commissioned the book, died in 1154. My own region of Abruzzo is famous for its *maccheroni alla chitarra* (guitar macaroni), so called because they are made on an ancient rectangular wooden instrument whose center is filled with strings like a guitar. On these strings the noodles (resembling square spaghetti) are cut. Nowadays a hand-cranked pasta machine cuts very acceptable *maccheroni alla chitarra*. Documentation about pasta in Italy is plentiful and can be found not only in cooking treatises, but also in history, literature, and even poetry. And indeed Italians do make their pastas into platefuls of poetry.

Basic Recipes for Homemade Pasta

I f pasta is to be served as a main dish, the rule is to use one egg per person, together with three-quarters cup of flour. However, as a first course, pasta made with four eggs will serve six people.

REGULAR PASTA

Serves 2 to 4
1¹/₂ cups all-purpose flour
2 large eggs

Serves 4 to 6
3 cups all-purpose flour
4 large eggs

WHOLE-WHEAT PASTA

1 cup whole-wheat flour
³/₄ cup all-purpose flour
2 large eggs

2 cups whole-wheat flour
¹/₂ cup all-pupose flour
4 large eggs

HOMEMADE
PASTA

NOTE: If necessary, dough can be prepared in advance. Wrap well in plastic or foil and refrigerate or freeze.

MAKING PASTA DOUGH
BY HAND

Place the flour in a mound in the middle of a pastry board or work surface. Dig a well in the center of the mound and break the eggs into it. Beat the eggs with a fork, and gradually start incorporating the flour into the eggs. You may or may not need all of the flour—it will depend on how much flour the eggs can absorb. As soon as you feel that you have a consistent bundle, start kneading the dough, using the palms of your hands. Using a pastry or dough scraper, scrape the board and incorporate all of the little pellets of dough. Continue kneading and folding the dough until you obtain a smooth, elastic ball. Knead for at least twenty minutes. If you are using a hand-cranked pasta machine, you do not need to work the dough this much; the kneading will be done by the machine. In either case, let the dough rest, covered with a bowl, for at least thirty minutes. This rest will give the gluten time to relax and make the dough easy to work.

MAKING GREEN PASTA
DOUGH BY HAND

Cook one-quarter pound of spinach (or half a package of frozen spinach) and wring out the spinach as much as possible. Very finely chop the spinach and add it to the eggs before you begin to incorporate the flour. Proceed as for making regular egg pasta by hand.

MAKING PASTA DOUGH IN A
FOOD PROCESSOR

Place the eggs in the bowl of a food processor. Turn the machine on and beat the eggs. Add one cup of flour and process, adding more flour until a ball of dough forms on the blades. If this doesn't happen and you get a mixture that resembles coarse meal, add a little bit of water and process until the ball of dough forms, or remove the dough to a pastry board and form a ball by kneading with your hands. Proceed as for handmade dough.

MAKING GREEN PASTA DOUGH WITH A FOOD PROCESSOR

Cook one-quarter pound of spinach (or half a package of frozen spinach) and wring out the spinach as much as possible. Very finely chop it and add to the eggs before you add any flour. Process until thoroughly combined and proceed as for making pasta dough in a food processor.

ROLLING OUT THE DOUGH BY HAND

Cut the dough into two or four parts, depending on the quantity of dough. Round and flatten each piece with your hands. Gently start to roll a rolling pin back and forth over the dough, and continue doing so until the dough is stretched to the desired thickness. Place the sheets of dough on clean tea towels to dry for about fifteen minutes.

Rolling out the dough by hand

CUTTING THE DOUGH BY HAND

Gently roll up each sheet of dough into a tube. Using a sharp knife, cut into the desired shape. If you want to make fettuccine, or *tagliatelle*, which are the same thing, cut across the rolled-up dough at one-eighth-inch intervals. You might want to use a ruler as your guide. If you want the noodles to have crinkled sides, cut the dough with a fluted pastry wheel. Unroll the strands of dough to their full length and dry on tea towels for up to one hour.

I do not recommend hanging the dough on a rack; the noodles usually break when removed. (But if you have a cat around, by all means use a rack; it will be difficult for the cat to take a walk on your pasta or to lie down in the middle of your *tagliatelle*.) If you plan to let the pasta dry for more than one hour, drape a napkin or tea towel over it. Store at room temperature.

Cutting the dough by hand

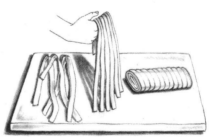

ROLLING OUT THE DOUGH WITH A HAND-OPERATED MACHINE

Cut the dough into two parts. Place the unused portion under a bowl. Flatten the other ball of pasta with your hands and divide it into two parts. Starting with the rollers as far apart as possible, insert the piece of dough between the two rollers of the machine. Turn the handle and roll the pasta through. Fold the dough into thirds and roll again. Knead the dough this way several times until smooth and not sticky, sprinkling the dough with flour as necessary.

Move the rollers one notch tighter and pass the dough without folding it through again. Keep tightening the space, one notch at a time, until the dough is the thickness you desire. Sprinkle the dough with flour if it seems sticky. If the dough begins to break when rolled through the cylinders, it needs more flour. Let the sheets of dough dry on a tea towel for fifteen minutes, but not longer; otherwise they become difficult to cut.

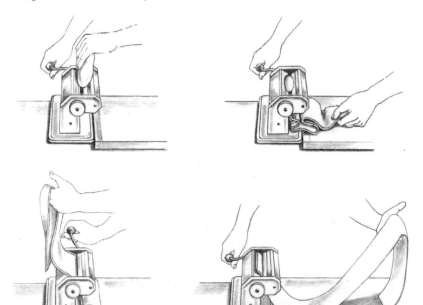

Rolling out the dough with a hand-operated machine

CUTTING THE PASTA WITH A HAND-OPERATED MACHINE

Choose the desired cutters according to size, and feed a sheet of dough into the machine. Unroll the strands to their full length and dry on tea towels for up to one hour. If you plan to let the pasta dry for more than one hour, drape a napkin or tea towel over it. Store at room temperature.

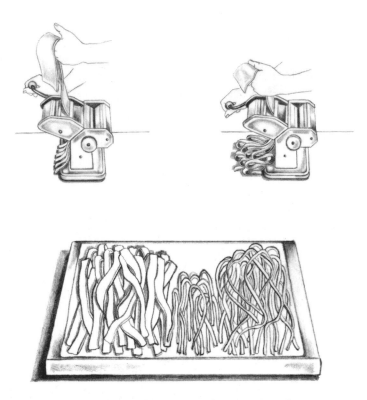

Cutting the dough with a hand-operated machine

COOKING PASTA

I have seen high prelates of gastronomy (even Italian, shame!) dumping pasta into an oil-spotted pot of boiling water. After the preliminary stirring, they wait for the water to come back to a boil *without covering the pot!* I know that my logic is often different from that of my husband and a few other people, but the more the pasta sits at the bottom of the pot waiting for the boiling motion to twirl it around and disengage the strands, the more the danger that it will become a tangled blob. Therefore, it should be logical to cover the pot so that the water can come back to a boil as soon as possible.

This is the process I prefer: For 1 pound of pasta, use a 5-quart pot. When the water boils, add a handful of coarse salt and let the water come back to a full boil. Add the pasta, stir, and cover the pot. When the steam starts to push up the lid of the pot, remove the lid, stir the pasta, and continue cooking with the lid askew. I place my long fork on the pot and set the lid on it. Pasta must cook quickly in constantly boiling water. If you follow these simple instructions, your pasta will cook perfectly and there will be no need to add oil.

ABOUT SAUCES

Remember, it is the sauce that makes the pasta fattening! So the lighter, the less rich or fatty your sauce, the better you will be at coping with a diet. Reserve the rich sauces that go better with homemade pasta for special occasions, and stick to what we Italians call the Mediterranean cuisine, based on fresh and seasonal ingredients, especially vegetables and fish. Give a second look to the tomato, which has been vilified lately but never abandoned. Used with a light touch, this delightful fruit will delicately dress a dish of pasta with its own juice. The addition of a few herbs, and just a touch of butter or oil, will do. (The virgin [green] olive oil, the juice of the olive, comes from a tree that in ancient Greece was sacred to Athena, the goddess of knowledge.)

ABOUT LEFTOVER COOKED PASTA

Reheat leftover pasta with a little oil or butter. For a wonderful meal, place the pasta in an ovenproof dish, beat one or two eggs with a sprinkling of minced fresh parsley, and pour on the pasta. Bake at 375° for twenty-five to thirty minutes. If the sauce does not contain fish, add some grated Parmesan cheese.

I detest pasta salads—a totally American invention that I hope will not surface in Italy—and cold pasta in general. However, I have included in this book one or two pasta dishes which can be eaten cold. But for heaven's sake, try not to refrigerate these pastas; the moment you do, you will ruin them. What makes cold pasta unappealing is its congealed sauce. If you must refrigerate, take the pasta out at least two hours before serving it. You will see the difference.

One word about colored pastas: We Italians use only spinach and red beets, and the purpose is just to achieve brilliant, definite color. We do not feel that tomatoes or carrots give a nice color to pasta, or any specific flavor. As for saffron pasta, what a waste of a good spice, and just to have a yellower pasta! Besides, if you add too much saffron, the pasta will taste awful. Keep your saffron for a good *risotto alla Milanese*. Another ingredient that should stay away from pasta is chocolate—maybe a little cocoa if you really like that color in your *tagliatelle*. Well, *de gustibus*, as the saying goes.

Glossary of Pasta

HOMEMADE PASTA

BIGOLI
Whole-wheat round noodles, similar to SPAGHETTI, extruded by a special hand-press pasta machine; a specialty from Veneto.

CANNELLONI
Broad, rectangular noodles about 3 × 5 inches, filled and rolled.

CAVATELLI
Small dumplings made with semolina and flour; a specialty from the south of Italy.

Cannelloni

Cavatelli

Chicche Verdi

CHICCHE VERDI

Little green dumplings made with potatoes and spinach; also called GNOCCHI VERDI, a specialty from Busseto, Verdi's native place in Emilia-Romagna.

FETTUCCINE

Thin noodles about ⅛ inch wide; also called TAGLIATELLE. FETTUCCINE VERDI are thin green noodles about ⅛ inch wide; also called TAGLIATELLE VERDI.

Fettuccine

GNOCCHI

Small dumplings, usually made with potatoes. GNOCCHI DI SEMOLINA. Small dumplings made with semolina; a Roman specialty. GNOCCHI VERDI. Small dumplings made with potatoes and spinach.

LASAGNE

Broad, thin noodles about 2–3 inches wide; also made commercially without eggs. LASAGNE VERDI. Broad, thin green noodles about 2–3 inches wide; also made commercially without eggs.

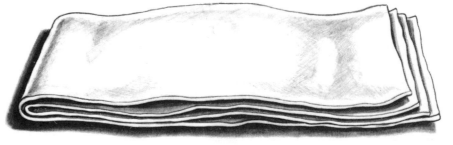

Lasagne

MACCHERONI ALLA CHITARRA

"Guitar" macaroni, the size of SPAGHETTI, cut on the strings of a rectangular wooden frame which resembles a guitar; a specialty of Abruzzo. They can also be cut with the narrow cutters of a pasta machine.

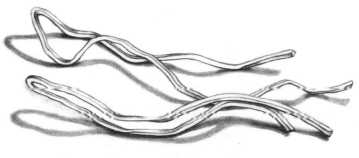

Maccheroni Alla Chitarra

MALTAGLIATI

Short-cut large noodles used especially for soups such as *pasta e fagioli*. The name means "bad cut," so if you wish, you can cut the noodles at random; I prefer them more or less the same length.

PAPPARDELLE

Broad noodles cut with a fluted pastry wheel to give them a crinkled edge. In Italy, they are traditionally served with hare sauce. Salsa alla Contadina (see page 41) or a Bolognese Sauce (page 38) would also be appropriate.

Pappardelle

QUADRUCCI
Made from TAGLIATELLE cut into small squares; always served in soup.

RAVIOLI
Little squares of dough about 2 › 2 inches, filled.

Ravioli

TAGLIATELLE
Thin noodles, about $1/8$ inch wide; also called FETTUCCINE. TAGLIATELLE VERDI. Thin green noodles about $1/8$ inch wide; also called FETTUCCINE VERDI.

TAGLIOLINI
Very fine, thin noodles, also called TAGLIERINI; often cooked in broth.

Tortellini

TORTELLINI
Little rounds of dough shaped like hats, stuffed; also called CAPPELLETTI, or little hats.

TROCCOLI
Large, square-cut noodles, $1/8 \times 1/8$ inch; a specialty of Apulia.

COMMERCIAL PASTA

PASTA LUNGA (long pasta)

BAVETTE. Another name for LINGUINE.

BUCATINI. SPAGHETTI with a hole in the middle.

LINGUINE. Flat SPAGHETTI, $^1/_8$ inch or less wide.

PERCIATELLI. SPAGHETTI with a hole; slightly thicker than BUCATINI.

SPAGHETTI. From the Italian word *spago*, literally "little cords"; solid strings of pasta.

SPAGHETTINI. Very fine SPAGHETTI.

TRENETTE. Similar to LINGUINE, sometimes a little wider; mostly used for *pesto* sauce; a specialty of Liguria.

Bucatini

Linguine

Spaghetti

PASTA CORTA (short pasta)

FARFALLE. Bow ties or butterflies.

FUSILLI. Corkscrews, about 1½ inches long. They also come in long shapes.

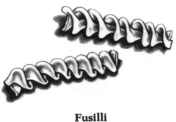

Fusilli

Farfalle

ORZO. Small pasta resembling barley.

PENNE. Quills; slant-cut macaroni.

RIGATONI. Grooved macaroni.

ROTELLE. Wheel-shaped macaroni.

TUBETTI. Little tubes, about ½ inch long.

ZITI. Even-cut macaroni, sometimes grooved.

ZITONI. Large ZITI.

Orzo

Penne

Rigatoni

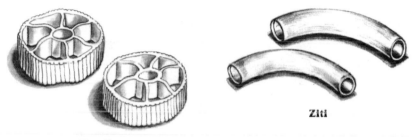

Rotelle

Ziti

SPECIAL CUT PASTA

Lasagne. Broad-cut thin pasta, 2–3 inches wide. It can also be green.

Lasagne ricce. Curly-edged Lasagne.

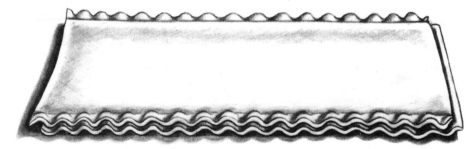

Lasagne Ricce

COMMERCIAL EGG PASTA

CAPELLI D'ANGELO. "Angel's hair"; very fine dry noodles. Also called CAPELLINI.

RAVIOLI. Dry ravioli.

TAGLIATELLE, or FETTUCCINE. Dry noodles.

TORTELLINI. Dry TORTELLINI.

Capelli d'Angelo

Tools and Utensils

Pasta can be made and cooked in any kitchen equipped with normal tools. However, I have found the following utensils to be particularly useful.

CHEESE GRATER
Many types of cheese graters are available. Use whichever kind suits you, but remember, you will be using it frequently.

Cheese Grater

COLANDER
A good colander is essential to any kitchen and is absolutely indispensable for draining pasta. Make sure you have a colander that will hold at least one pound of pasta.

DOUGH OR PASTRY SCRAPER
A dough scraper, a small stainless-steel blade with a wooden handle, is indispensable for pulling together all the excess pieces of dough as you work.

FOOD MILL
The food mill will never be obsolete, no matter how sophisticated the food processor becomes. Use it to strain your sauces, especially tomato sauces. If tomato seeds are crushed (as they are

Dough Scraper

23

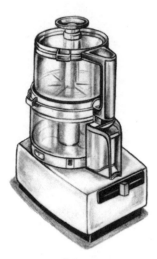

Food Processor

with a food processor or blender), the sauce will be bitter. With a food mill, the seeds remain intact while the sauce is strained through. To my mind, a food mill is one tool no kitchen should be without.

FOOD PROCESSOR OR BLENDER
Throughout this book, I have recommended that ingredients be combined in a food processor or blender. I find my food processor has become my right arm, and if you must purchase either a food processor or blender, I strongly urge that you buy the processor. It is far more versatile and is effective in kneading pasta dough.

GARLIC PRESS
I find this gadget quite useful for puréeing garlic when you need to mix it thoroughly in a sauce or dressing.

Garlic Press

KNIVES
To my mind, investing in a good chef's knife is basic for any kind of cooking. You will also need a paring knife.

PASTA BOWLS AND SERVING PLATTERS
For serving pasta, you will need a large, shallow bowl. Never serve pasta in a deep bowl, because the sauce will collect in the bottom. Spaghetti, in fact, is better served on a flat platter.

PASTA MACHINES
There are several brands of pasta machines on the market. The fancy electric ones mix, knead, and extrude pasta of virtually every shape. They certainly make less work, but the results are not always satisfactory. A food processor and a hand-cranked pasta machine are all you need.

I prefer the hand-cranked machine that makes several thicknesses of pasta sheets and also is equipped with several cutting rollers. Pasta machines can be purchased at gourmet kitchenware stores.

Pasta Machine

PASTA WHEELS AND CUTTERS

For the recipes in this book, you will need a straight-edged wheel for cutting tortellini and other similar pastas, and a fluted-edged wheel for cutting ravioli, lasagna, and *pappardelle* noodles. There are also individual tortellini cutters that are very good.

Pasta Wheels   **Ravioli Cutter**

PASTRY BOARD

A pastry board is vital to making pasta. In Italy, it is always set on a marble table, and is an integral part of the Italian kitchen.

PIZZELLE IRON OR MACHINE

This is similar to a waffle iron and makes two *pizzelle* at a time.

POTS AND PANS

To cook any kind of pasta, you'll need a large pot, at least five-quarts in capacity, and a pot lid. The pot should be made from material that conducts heat easily, such as cast iron or even a less expensive aluminum.

For sauces, you will need a heavy saucepan, 1½-quart to 2½-quart capacity. You will also need a skillet; the nine-inch variety is probably the most versatile.

RAVIOLI TRAYS

Ravioli trays or forms, sold in gourmet shops, are handy and make ravioli making much easier. However, they are not a necessity.

ROLLING PIN

Wooden rolling pins work best, in my experience. Be sure to season a new rolling pin with olive oil before using it.

WOODEN FORKS AND SPOONS

A long-handled wooden fork, which in Italy is called a *forchettone*, is essential for untangling spaghetti. A long-handled wooden spoon is equally essential for stirring pasta, and shorter wooden spoons are needed for stirring sauces.

Forchettone

Ingredients

The following are ingredients you will need for recipes in this book.

ANCHOVIES
These fish fillets are packed in olive oil or salt. They are used in antipasto and for some sauces. Anchovy paste can be used as a substitute.

ARTICHOKES
Only the very small, baby artichokes are used in this book. Frozen artichoke hearts are a good substitute for fresh ones since it is difficult to find artichokes so small that a choke has not yet developed.

BOUILLON CUBES
A godsend when broth is not available. I prefer the chicken-flavored cubes for their more delicate flavor. Canned broth, diluted with water to cut the saltiness, is also a good substitute. You might want to try low-sodium broth.

BREAD CRUMBS
Buy unseasoned bread crumbs and add your own seasoning, or make your own bread crumbs by drying bread in a slow oven and crumbling it in a food processor or blender.

BUTTER

Use sweet, unsalted butter. Butter is salted to ensure a long shelf life; therefore, salted butter is less fresh than the unsalted type.

CAPERS

Capers are the flower bud of a Mediterranean plant. They come packed in salt (rinse before using) or vinegar, and are wonderful for flavoring certain sauces and dishes.

CHOCOLATE

Use good-quality bitter or bittersweet chocolate. Good brands are Callebaut, Lindt, Maillard, Ghirardelli, Perugina, Suchard, Tobler, Van Houten, and, in a pinch, good old reliable Baker's.

CLOVES

Used especially to flavor broth and some sauces. Use cloves carefully; their aroma can be overpowering.

COCOA POWDER

I think that Droste, Perugina, and Nestlé are very good brands.

FLOUR

Unless specified, the flour used in this book is all-purpose Hecker's flour. It is unbleached and has a good percentage of durum wheat and more gluten, which is essential for high-quality homemade pasta.

GARLIC

Buy garlic fresh, one bulb at a time, and keep it in a little basket or crock, away from light. Choose heads that are white and firm. Garlic must be used with discretion, unless you are making a *pesto* sauce or something especially garlicky.

HERBS

Basil is a beautiful garden herb. Nowadays, greengrocers sell basil all year round. In winter, when basil is expensive, dried basil is a good substitute as a flavoring. Basil is used mainly in tomato sauces and salads; it is the main ingredient in *pesto* (see page 114).
Bay leaves are excellent for grilled meats, stews, and roasts.
Marjoram is similar to oregano but more delicate. It is used, fresh or dried, in sauces and with meats and fish.
Mint is used mostly fresh, with lamb and vegetables.
Oregano is more pungent than marjoram. Oregano is excellent in dried form.
Parsley: always use fresh Italian, flat-leaf parsley. The flat leaves

seem to me to be more flavorful. When dried, parsley is totally useless; it will ruin a dish and is the only herb that is awful dried.
Rosemary: perhaps my favorite herb. Excellent with chicken, rabbit, lamb, pork, and vegetables, especially bell peppers.
Sage is wonderful when fresh, on veal and in butter sauces. Dried sage is fine but not preferred.

MUSHROOMS

When the *porcini* mushrooms are in season in Italy and a basket of them is brought into the kitchen, their aroma permeates the entire room. White American button mushrooms do not have much flavor, although now we also have golden oak mushrooms and other native species that are quite good and have a wonderful texture. A good way to improve the flavor when cooking fresh mushrooms is to add one or two tablespoons of dried *porcini*. They are expensive, but a small bundle goes a long way.

MUSTARD

Many types of mustards are available. I prefer Dijon or Pommery, which is grainy.

NUTMEG

Like cloves, this is a very heady spice. When used with discretion, it imparts a delicate aroma to sauces, especially Béchamel Sauce (see page 42).

OLIVE OIL

Extra-virgin olive oil (*olio extra vergine di oliva*) is the pure juice of the first pressing of the olive, filtered through cheesecloth. When used for cooking, it imparts a special flavor. I use it for everything; when frying, I combine it with peanut oil and get excellent results. My favorite brands are Amore, Colavita, and Amastra from the south, and those from Tuscany such as Ruffino, Badia a Coltibuono, and Olivieri. Store olive oil in a dark cool place, not in the refrigerator. Remember that before there was refrigeration, olive oil was used to preserve food.

PANCETTA

Appearing more and more frequently in Italian recipes, *pancetta* is bacon that is salt-cured, not smoked. It is used in sauces, with pasta, and with vegetables. Sometimes American bacon can be substituted for it.

PROSCIUTTO

There are two types of prosciutto in Italy. *Prosciutto crudo* (raw) is cured unsmoked ham; *prosciutto cotto* is baked or boiled ham.

Prosciutto should be slightly moist and not too salty. The best is from Parma, but no Italian prosciutto can be imported into the United States. Fortunately, we have local firms such as Citterio, Volpi, and Daniele, which make very good products. Hormel is also quite good.

RED PEPPERS

Peperoncino, hot peppers, or *diavoletto* (little devil, as it is called in Abruzzo) are sold whole, dried, or fresh in Italy. Here they are more available crushed. Lately, however, I have seen bunches of fresh little peppers in some of the produce markets that are sprouting up all over New York. Buy them and hang them in the kitchen to dry. They are also quite decorative.

RICE

For a *risotto*, use Arborio imported Italian rice. I find that long-grain American rice is excellent in preparations such as *timballi* or casseroles.

SAFFRON

The dried stigma of the crocus is one of the most expensive spices in the world. To make one kilogram of saffron, 400 kilos of hand-harvested threads are needed. Fortunately, a little goes a long way; in fact, too much saffron is not pleasant. I prefer the powdered type from L'Aquila, Italy. Saffron is used for coloring and flavor; it is a must in *risotto alla Milanese*.

SEMOLINA

Finely ground durum wheat.

TOMATOES

There is nothing better than a good *sugo di pomodoro*, a tomato sauce made with fresh ripe tomatoes. But alas, good tomatoes are available only in the middle of the summer. Canned tomatoes are a useful substitute; the best are those from San Marzano, Italy, but I find that the American, especially Californian, brands are quite good. Do not buy ground or crushed tomatoes; strain your canned or fresh tomatoes with a food mill to keep the seeds from being crushed. Since the crushed seeds will make the sauce bitter, you might want to add the whole tomato. Go ahead; the seeds, uncrushed, will not spoil the sauce. It will just be a bit more rustic. Sun-dried tomatoes are used in some recipes. They are available in Italian or specialty food shops.

TOMATO PASTE

We Italians use tomato paste for flavor and color and we measure

it with a teaspoon! Only occasionally is a large quantity of tomato paste used, as in Bolognese Sauce (see page 38), but then it
is diluted with quite a bit of broth. Too much paste will make a
sauce harsh and heavy.

TRUFFLES

Truffles are rare and expensive, especially the fresh, white ones
from Italy. But once you try them, you will never use the canned
type again. One truffle goes a long way. They are excellent on *tagliatelle* or tortellini and many other dishes.

TUNA

Italian tunafish is packed in olive oil, and I use it exclusively. It
is excellent for sauces.

VINEGAR

In Italy, you are never asked which salad dressing you want on
your salad; there is only one: vinegar and oil. Vinegar is almost
always wine vinegar and usually is red. Balsamic vinegars are
more delicate, aromatic, and mellow than the regular ones, and
the flavor does not interfere much with wine. We dress salads
with other condiments, but they have a name of their own as in
Insalata alla Siciliana (see page 172).

A FEW WORDS ABOUT CHEESE

FONTINA

The best Fontina comes from Val d'Aosta in Piedmont. It is a
good cheese to eat, and is excellent for melting.

MOZZARELLA

I use mozzarella a lot. It is a light, mild cheese that is excellent
for a snack by itself and in combination with prosciutto, ham,
salami, and the like. The best is the freshly made whole-milk
mozzarella. The partly skimmed is not very flavorful, to my
mind, but if you need to cut down on fat, use it. In recent years
buffalo-milk mozzarella has appeared on the American scene; it
is expensive, but what a flavor it has!

PARMESAN

The best Parmesan comes from the provinces of Reggio Emilia,
Parma, Modena, and Bologna. It is mainly a cheese for grating,
but Reggiano is excellent as an eating cheese. The *grana Padana*
is a type of Parmesan that is a little drier, also good for grating,
and a little less expensive. To keep in the refrigerator, wrap in

dampened cheesecloth and place in a plastic container. Check it often and if mildew appears, just remove the mildew. You can also freeze it in pieces, but wrap well. Grated Parmesan keeps very well in the freezer. If you do not use Parmesan often, it is advisable to grate it and freeze it.

PECORINO
This cheese is better known as Romano in this country, although there is also the well known Pecorino Sardo, which is equally good. Almost every region in Italy has its own Pecorino. They are hard cheeses made from sheep's milk. Thet are a little sharp, and are used in certain pasta dishes.

RICOTTA
This is a soft, fresh, delicately flavored, creamy cheese made from ewe's milk. It is used mostly for stuffing, although ricotta is excellent by itself and wonderful for sweet desserts.

SWISS OR EMMENTALER
These cheeses are used often in Italian cooking, as is French Gruyère. Don't be surprised when you see them listed in the ingredients.

A FEW WORDS ABOUT WINE

An Italian meal is incomplete if not accompanied with wine, *vino da tavola*, locally produced table wine for everyday use, or a bottle of quality wine for special occasions and guests.

I am not a wine expert so I will not give you a long speech. I choose my wines to complement the food I am serving, and I go very much according to my taste. So should you. If you feel insecure about selecting a wine for your dinner, ask for advice at your local wine shop. However, to help you with the menus in this book, I do suggest appropriate wines.

When selecting Italian wines, the best are those marked D.O.C., which means Denominazione di Origine Controllata. Special laws control the authenticity of the place of origin, the grape type, vinification method, aging, and alcohol level. D.O.C.G. laws more strictly control certain high-quality wine types such as Vino Nobile di Montepulciano, Brunello di Montalcino, Barbaresco, and Barolo. These bottlings are among the finest Italy has to offer. But there are many wines that are inexpensive and good even though they do not have a particular designation. Try a bottle, and if you like it, stock up on it.

Some Helpful Hints

- *Prosciutto* is more flavorful than ham. When a recipe calls for chopped prosciutto, ask your grocer to sell you an end piece; it is less expensive and excellent for stuffings.
- *To peel tomatoes*, pour boiling water on them, then let them cool a little. The skin will come off very easily.
- *To roast peppers*, just place directly on the gas flame and turn often so that the skin is completely charred. Dump into a brown bag, close tightly, and cool. This will make the peeling easier.
- *When frying*, add a piece of bread soaked in vinegar to the hot oil. This will purify the oil; when the bread floats to the surface, the oil is ready. Fried food keeps well for thirty to forty-five minutes in a switched-off oven or one with a pilot light.
- *When making broth*, freeze some of the strained liquid in ice-cube trays. It will be handy when you need a small quantity for a sauce or a sauté.
- *Before cooking mussels* or clams, place them in cool water and sprinkle one tablespoon of flour over. This will drain the sand out of the mollusks.
- *To wash vegetables* with a lot of sand attached, soak them for five to ten minutes in tepid water to which a tablespoon of kosher or coarse salt has been added.

- *Basil leaves* should not be chopped, if possible. Just tear them into little pieces with your fingers; they will not turn brown.
- *Dry parsley* is useless; use fresh parsley all the time. If not available, omit it or use another herb, even if dry.
- *Leftover egg whites* freeze quite well. You can also use ice-cube trays. Defrost at room temperature.
- *When decorating a cake*, place strips of wax paper underneath the cake and remove them when you finish. This will prevent soiled doilies and serving dishes.
- *When draining pasta*, reserve one cup of the cooking water. With certain sauces—creamy ones, for instance—pasta may look too dry and a little of the reserved water will make it moist without adding more cream or butter.
- *Leftover pasta* can be reheated in the oven. You can also make a nice *frittata:* to one cup of pasta, add one beaten egg and some Parmesan cheese, then bake until hot. Or make a little *timbale* by layering your pasta with mozzarella. If pasta is dressed with a fish sauce, omit the cheese and egg, and warm up in a double boiler.
- *Quantities for salt*, pepper, herbs, and spices are often omitted from a recipe; that means you should use them to your own taste.

Basic Sauces

A sauce (*salsa* or *sugo* in Italian) is meant to complement pasta; it should not overwhelm it. What makes pasta fattening is the type of sauce you put on it. The lighter the sauce, the better your diet. Vegetable and meatless tomato sauces are the most healthful. When on a diet, make a tomato sauce without oil, butter, or salt—the taste of the tomatoes plus a sprinkling of your favorite herbs and a touch of garlic or onion make a flavorful combination.

For that moment when a yearning for spaghetti hits you, just toss the drained strands with a tablespoon of fresh butter and a handful of Parmesan cheese. It will make a delicious, light dish that will nevertheless satisfy a hearty appetite.

SUGO FINTO
Tomato Sauce
Makes 2 cups

Sugo finto, literally "fake sauce," is the name given to a tomato sauce without meat.

¼ cup olive oil
2 tablespoons unsalted butter
1 small onion, chopped
1 small carrot, chopped
1 celery rib, chopped
2 pounds fresh tomatoes, peeled and seeded, or 2 cups canned tomato purée
1 parsley sprig, minced
2 to 3 fresh basil leaves or a pinch of dried basil
Salt and freshly ground pepper

1. In a saucepan, combine the oil and 1 tablespoon of the butter over moderate heat. Add the onion, carrot, and celery and cook, stirring, for about 10 minutes.
2. Add the tomatoes, parsley, and basil and season with salt and pepper to taste. Bring to a boil, cover, and cook over moderately low heat for 30 minutes. Remove from the heat and stir in the remaining 1 tablespoon butter. Serve at once or reheat over low heat.

NOTE: This sauce freezes well.

AGLIO E OLIO
Garlic and Oil Sauce
To dress 1 pound of spaghetti or linguine

¼ cup olive oil
2 garlic cloves
A few flakes of *diavoletto* (hot red pepper flakes)
2 tablespoons minced fresh parsley

1. In a saucepan, combine the oil, garlic, and *diavoletto* over moderate heat. As soon as the garlic begins to sizzle, add 1 tablespoon of the parsley. Sauté for a few seconds.
2. Pour the sauce over the pasta and sprinkle with the remaining 1 tablespoon parsley. Serve at once.

1 large garlic clove, peeled and slightly crushed
2 parsley sprigs
4 to 5 fresh basil leaves or a pinch of oregano
A few flakes of *diavoletto* (red hot pepper flakes)
1/4 cup plus 1 tablespoon olive oil
1 teaspoon tomato paste
1 pound fresh tomatoes, peeled and seeded, or 1 can (16 ounces) peeled tomatoes, drained

In a heavy saucepan, combine all of the ingredients over moderate heat. Bring to a boil, reduce the heat to low, and simmer for 15 to 20 minutes. Discard the parsley and garlic and pour the sauce over freshly cooked pasta.

NOTE: This sauce can be prepared in large batches and frozen.

1/2 pound *mascarpone* cheese or 1 large package (8 ounces) cream cheese, at room temperature
1/2 cup loosely packed torn basil leaves, or 1/2 teaspoon oregano
1/2 cup minced fresh parsley
1/4 cup Bolognese Sauce (see page 38) or other red sauce (optional)
1 garlic clove, minced
3/4 cup heavy cream
1 pound pasta
Freshly grated Parmesan, Pecorino Romano, or Sardo cheese

1. In a pasta serving bowl, combine the *mascarpone* or cream cheese, herbs, sauce, if used, garlic, and cream.
2. In a large pot of salted boiling water, cook the pasta according to package directions, until just *al dente*. Drain the pasta, reserving 1 cup of the cooking water. Turn the pasta into the bowl with the sauce. Toss, adding as much water as necessary to make the sauce and pasta creamy and smooth, but not soupy.
3. Serve hot and pass the freshly grated cheese.

SUGO ALLA BOLOGNESE
Bolognese Sauce
Serves 6

This sauce is excellent for all sorts of noodles, spaghetti, and macaroni.

1 slice prosciutto, $1/4$ inch thick, cubed
1 parsley sprig
1 medium onion, quartered
1 celery rib, quartered
1 medium carrot, quartered
3 tablespoons olive oil
1 tablespoon unsalted butter
1 pound beef, veal, and pork, chopped together
1 fresh sage leaf or $1/4$ teaspoon dried sage
Salt and freshly ground pepper
$1/4$ cup dry wine
3 tablespoons tomato paste
2 cups chicken or beef broth
$1/4$ cup heavy cream

1. In a food processor or blender, combine the prosciutto, parsley, onion, celery, and carrot. Process until the mixture is the consistency of cream.
2. In a saucepan, combine the oil and butter over moderate heat. Add the vegetable mixture and cook, stirring, until slightly browned. Stir in the meat and sage. Cook, stirring frequently, until quite brown.
3. Season to taste with salt and pepper. Add the wine and cook until it evaporates. Blend the tomato paste with the broth and stir it into the sauce. Cover and simmer, stirring occasionally, for about 1 hour. Remove from the heat and add the cream.

This sauce, which is similar to Bolognese Sauce (see page 38), is good for all kinds of stuffed pasta, such as cannelloni, ravioli, or lasagne.

SUGO DI CARNE
Meat Sauce
Serves 6

1 slice prosciutto, ¼ inch thick, cubed
1 parsley sprig
1 medium onion, quartered
1 celery rib, quartered
1 medium carrot, quartered
3 tablespoons olive oil
2 tablespoons unsalted butter
1 pound beef, veal, and pork, chopped together
¼ teaspoon dried sage
Salt and freshly ground pepper
¼ cup dry wine
1 tablespoon tomato paste
2 cans (16 ounces each) tomato purée
1 fresh basil leaf or a pinch of dried basil

1. In a food processor or blender, combine the prosciutto, parsley, onion, celery, and carrot. Process until the mixture is the consistency of cream.
2. In a saucepan, combine the oil and 1 tablespoon of the butter over moderate heat. Add the vegetable mixture and cook, stirring, until slightly browned. Stir in the meat and sage and cook, stirring frequently, until quite brown.
3. Season to taste with salt and pepper. Add the wine and cook until it evaporates. Stir in the tomato paste, tomato purée, and basil. Simmer, stirring occasionally, for 1¼ hours. Remove from the heat and add the remaining 1 tablespoon butter.

RAGÙ ALL' ITALIANA
Meat Sauce for Pasta
Makes about 9 cups

¼ cup plus 2 tablespoons olive oil
2 medium onions
1 celery rib, halved
1 carrot, quartered
1 parsley sprig
1 pound beef chuck or rump
1 pound pork shoulder
2 to 3 Italian sweet sausages
1 pound veal shoulder
Salt and freshly ground pepper
1 cup dry wine
¼ cup plus 2 tablespoons tomato paste
3 pounds fresh tomatoes, peeled and seeded, or 2 cans (32 ounces each) peeled tomatoes
1 to 2 fresh basil leaves or a large pinch of dried basil

1. In a large heavy casserole, warm the oil over moderate heat. Cut a cross at the bottom of each onion and add to the casserole together with the remaining *odori di cucina* ("perfume of the kitchen"): the celery, carrot, and parsley. Sauté briefly and add the beef, pork, sausages, and veal. Pierce the sausages with the tip of a sharp knife and cook until all of the meats are well browned.

2. Season the mixture with salt and pepper to taste. Add the wine and cook until it evaporates. Add the tomato paste, tomatoes, and basil. Stir well, cover, reduce the heat to very low, and cook until the meats are tender, about 2½ hours. Use the sauce to dress any kind of pasta.

NOTE: This sauce freezes beautifully.

¼ **pound dried tomatoes, coarsely chopped**
2 onions, chopped
1 garlic clove, minced
4 tablespoons olive oil
1 teaspoon tomato paste
¼ **cup wine or water**
A few flakes of *diavoletto* (hot red pepper flakes, optional)
Salt and freshly ground pepper
2 to 3 parsley sprigs, minced

1. In a large skillet, combine the tomatoes, onions, garlic, and 2 tablespoons of the oil. Cover and cook over low heat, stirring from time to time, for about 20 minutes.

2. Dilute the tomato paste with the wine and add it to the skillet. Add the *diavoletto*, if used, and season to taste with salt and pepper. Cover and cook over low heat until the tomatoes and onions are tender, 25 to 30 minutes. Add the remaining 2 tablespoons oil and remove from the heat.

3. Pour the sauce on freshly cooked pasta and sprinkle with the parsley.

MAYONNAISE
Makes 1 cup

1 egg
Pinch of salt
½ **teaspoon dry mustard**
1 tablespoon wine vinegar
¾ **cup olive oil**
Lemon juice

1. In a food processor or blender, combine the egg, salt, dry mustard, and vinegar. Process until well blended. Begin to add the oil, drop by drop, until the ingredients form an emulsion. Add the remaining oil in a light stream until thoroughly consolidated into a mayonnaise. Season with lemon juice to taste.

2. Store the mayonnaise, covered, in the refrigerator for up to one week.

SALSA BALSAMELLA
Béchamel Sauce
Makes 1 cup

1 tablespoon unsalted butter
1 heaping tablespoon all-purpose flour
1 cup milk
Pinch of salt
Pinch of white pepper

In a heavy saucepan, melt the butter over moderate heat. Add the flour and cook, stirring, for a few minutes. Off the heat, add the milk, a little at a time, whisking constantly until the sauce liquefies. Place over moderate heat and cook, whisking constantly, until the sauce thickens and begins to "puff." Let the sauce puff once or twice and remove from the heat. Season to taste with the salt and pepper.

NOTE: If a recipe calls for a thicker béchamel, add more flour at the beginning.

THE MENUS

Preface to Menus

In preparing the menus for this book, I tried to escape the obvious, well-known pasta dishes whose recipes can be found in other cookbooks. I balanced the menus according to the ingredients, but I didn't mind constructing some menus based entirely on fish, vegetables, or meat.

Naturally, the reader can substitute dishes at will and according to personal taste. The menus and the recipes have been tried several times in my cooking school, where the sessions of the pasta course are geared to showcase a pasta entree, preceded by an appropriate antipasto and accompanied by a suitable salad and dessert.

I wish to stress that serving pasta as a main dish is *not* the traditional Italian way. Pasta in Italy is always served as a first course, to be followed by a main dish of meat or fish with accompanying vegetables. Americans have learned to cook and love pasta, and they like to eat it as a main dish. So be it! I do not think it is such a bad idea.

An Italian dinner always ends with fruit. Sweet desserts are reserved for Sunday dinners and special occasions. However, when in New York, Boston, Seattle, or Los Angeles, let's eat cake—at least sometimes. *Buon appetito!*

Menus for Spring

PANE E SALAME
Bread and Salami

ZUPPA DI VERDURE ALLA GENOVESE
Genoa-Style Vegetable Soup

INSALATA DI TONNO MAMMA E PAPÀ
Mother and Father's Tuna Salad

BUDINO DI RICOTTA
Ricotta Pudding

Wine: Trebbiano d'Abruzzo

———

PESCE ALLE OLIVE E CAPPERI
Fish with Olives and Capers

SPAGHETTI ALLA CARBONARA
Spaghetti Tossed with Bacon, Butter, Eggs, and Cheese

INSALATA ALLA SIRACUSANA
Syracusa-Style Salad

MARGHERITA DI FRUTTA ALL'ITALIANA
Italian-Style Fruit Marguerite

Wine: Barbaresco

ASPARAGI AL PROSCIUTTO COTTO
Ham-Wrapped Asparagus

PASTA CON RAGÙ D'AGNELLO E PEPERONI
ALL'ABRUZZESE
Pasta with Lamb and Pepper Ragout Abruzzo Style

INSALATA DI DUE FAGIOLI
Two-Bean Salad

FRAGOLE IN SPUMA ROSE
Strawberries in Pink Foam

Wine: Montepulciano d'Abruzzo

———

CROSTONI AI FUNGHI
Mushroom Toasts

TAGLIATELLE VERDI AL SALMONE
Green Noodles with Salmon

INSALATA DI BROCCOLI, POMODORI, E
CETRIOLI AL GORGONZOLA
Broccoli, Tomato, and Cucumber Salad with
Gorgonzola

BISCOTTINI ALL'UVETTA
Little Raisin Cookies

Wine: Soave

———

FUNGHI FARCITI AL PROSCIUTTO COTTE E
SALAME
Stuffed Mushrooms with Ham and Salami

PASTA DEL FATTORE
Farmer's Pasta

INSALATA GIORNALIERA
Everyday Salad

SPUMONE ALL'AURUM
Golden Froth

Wine: Rosatello

―――

CAPESANTE AL PESTO
Scallops with Pesto

FARFALLE ROMANTICHE
Romantic Butterflies

INSALATA DI RAPE ROSSE ED ARUGOLA
Beet and Arugula Salad

SPUMONE ALL'AURUM
Golden Froth

Wine: Galestro

―――

CAPONATA ALLA SICILIANA CON SALSA SAN BERNARDO
Sicilian Caponata with San Bernardo Sauce

LASAGNE IN BRODO ALLA LANCIANESE
Lasagna in Broth Lanciano Style

INSALATA CROCCANTE
Crunchy Salad

CROSTATA DI CREMA JOLANDA
Jolanda's Cream Pie

Wine: Bardolino

―――

ANTIPASTO ALLA MARINARA
Mariner's Antipasto

TAGLIOLINI AI QUATTRO FORMAGGI
Noodles with Four Cheeses

INSALATA GIORNALIERA
Everyday Salad

TORTA ALLE MORE
Blackberry Cake

Wine: Chianti Classico

———

ZUCCHINE A SCAPECE
Marinated Zucchini

CANNELLONI ALL'ETRUSCA
Cannelloni with Mushrooms, Ham, and Cheese

INSALATA DI TONNO MAMMA E PAPÀ
Mother and Father's Tuna Salad

PERE ALLA GABRIELLA
Pears Gabriella

Wine: Galestro

———

ANTIPASTO DI FEGATINI ALL'ABRUZZESE
Chicken Livers Abruzzo Style

SPAGHETTI PRIMAVERA
Springtime Spaghetti

INSALATA ALLA NEVE
Snowy Salad

TORTA DI CIOCCOLATA ALLE NOCI
Chocolate Cake with Walnuts

Wine: Rosso del Conero

UOVA DELICATE
Melt-in-the-Mouth Eggs

LINGUINE DEL PESCATORE
Fisherman's Linguine

MELANZANE ALLA BARESE
Bari-Style Eggplant

CASSATA CASALINGA ALLA SICILIANA
Homemade Sicilian Cassata

Wine: Bianco dell'Etna

TRADITIONAL DISHES FOR EASTER

UOVA AL CAVIALE
Eggs with Caviar

TIMBALLO DI ZITONI ALL'IMPIEDI
Standing Ziti Timbale

INSALATA ROSATA DI FAGIOLINI
Beet and String Bean Salad

MACEDONIA DI FRUTTA
Fruit Melange

Wine: Fiano Bianco di Avellino

Menus for Summer

TORTINO FANTASIA
Baked Frittata

PASTA AL PESTO
Pasta with Pesto

INSALATA DI CALPURNIA
Calpurnia's Salad

BUDINO DI CIOCCOLATA
Chocolate Pudding

Wine: Collio Bianco

———

ANTIPASTO DI MOZZARELLA ALL'ERBETTE
Mozzarella Antipasto with Herbs

SPAGHETTI ALLA PUTTANESCA LIA SARACENI
Lia Saraceni's Spaghetti with Harlots' Sauce

INSALATA DI RAPE ROSSE ED ARUGOLA
Beet and Arugula Salad

CROSTATA DI PESCHE CON RICOTTA
Peach and Ricotta Pie

Wine: Tocai del Friule

AVOCADO AL TONNO
Avocados with Tunafish

PASTA ALLA NERANO
Nerano-Style Pasta

LA CAPRESE
Capri-Style Salad

ZUPPA INGLESE CASA MIA
Home-Style Zuppa Inglese

Wine: Fiano Bianco di Avellino

━━━

ANTIPASTO DI POLPI
Octopus Antipasto

PASTA CON LA SALSA CRUDA
Pasta with Uncooked Sauce

PEPERONI ARROSTITI
Roasted Peppers

ZABAGLIONE CLASSICO
Classic Zabaglione

Wine: Corvo Bianco

━━━

SALSICCE ALLO SPIEDO
Skewered Sausages

**MACCHERONI COL SUGHETTO ACERBO ALLA
LELLA**
Macaroni with Green and Red Sauce Lella

INSALATA CROCCANTE
Crunchy Salad

SORBETTO DI ALBICOCCHE AL VOV
Apricot Sherbet with Vov

Wine: Montepulciano d'Abruzzo

POLLO AL VERDE
Green Chicken

MACCHERONI AI QUATTRO FORMAGGI
Macaroni with Four Cheeses

INSALATA GENOVESE
Genoa-Style Salad

CREMA DI FRUTTA ERMIONE
Fruit Cream Hermione

Wine: Pinot Grigio

━━━━━

POMODORI ALL'ADRIATICA
Tomatoes Adriatic

TAGLIATELLE AL LIMONE
Tagliatelle with Lemon

PANZANELLA DELLA CASA
Bread Salad

SUSINE ALLA CREMA
Plums with Custard

Wine: Galestro

━━━━━

BACCALÀ TRICOLORE
Tricolored Baccalà

PAGLIA E FIENO ALLA ANNA TERESA
Straw and Hay à la Anna Teresa

MELANZANE MEDITERRANEE
Mediterranean Eggplant

PIZZELLE ALLA GUARDIESE
Pizzelle à la Guardiagrele

Wine: Verdicchio

ANTIPASTO DI MOZZARELLA ALL'ERBETTE
Mozzarella Antipasto with Herbs

GNOCCHI DI PATATE TRICOLORE
Tricolored Potato Gnocchi

ASPARAGI AL LIMONE
Asparagus with Lemon

PESCHE AL LAMBRUSCO
Peaches with Lambrusco Wine

Wine: Orvieto

▬▬

ANTIPASTO ALLA GIULIESE
Antipasto à la Giulianova

GNOCCHI DI SEMOLINA ALLA ROMANA
Roman-Style Semolina Gnocchi

INSALATA DI POMODORI E CETRIOLI
Tomato and Cucumber Salad

GRANITA DI CAFFÈ
Coffee Ice

Wine: Rosatello

▬▬

MOZZARELLE IN CARROZZA CON ACCIUGHE
Fried Mozzarella and Anchovy Sandwiches

TORTELLINI DELL'ESTATE
Summer Tortellini

INSALATA DI ARUGOLA E INDIVIA BELGA
Arugula and Belgian Endive Salad

ARANCE E KIWI ALL'AMARETTO
Oranges and Kiwis with Amaretto

Wine: Sassella

COZZE CON LA SALSA VERDE
Mussels in Green Sauce

CANNELLONI ALLA ANNA TERESA
Anna Teresa's Cannelloni

INSALATA DI FAGIOLINI MIMOSA
String Bean Salad Mimosa

SORBETTO DI ALBICOCCHE AL VOV
Apricot Sherbet with Vov

Wine: Verdicchio

━━━

FUNGHI RIPIENI AI CAPPERI
Stuffed Mushrooms with Capers

PASTICCIO DI LASAGNE RICCE AL SALMONE
Curly Lasagna Timbale with Salmon

INSALATA ALLA SICILIANA
Sicilian-Style Salad

PESCHE AL LAMBRUSCO
Peaches with Lambrusco Wine

Wine: Verdicchio

A SUMMER PICNIC

VITELLO TONNATO
Tunnied Veal

PASTA DELL'ESTATE
Summer Pasta

INSALATA COLORATA
Colorful Salad

SPUMA DI PESCHE AL RUM
Cold Peach Soufflé with Rum

Wine: Lambrusco di Sorbara

Menus for Autumn

TORTA DEL PESCATORE
Fisherman's Pie

SPAGHETTI ALLA CONTADINA
Spaghetti Peasant Style

INSALATA DI ZUCCHINE
Zucchini Salad

BISCOTTINI ALL'UVETTA
Little Raisin Cookies

Wine: Brolio Bianco

FUNGHETTI MARINATI
Marinated Mushrooms

PASTA ALL'AMATRICIANA
Amatrice-Style Pasta

INSALATA ALLA SICILIANA
Sicilian-Style Salad

SEMIFREDDO DI FRAGOLE
Strawberry Mousse

Wine: Gattinara

CIAMBOTTA DI FEDERICO SPERA
Fried Vegetables Federico Spera

LINGUINE O SPAGHETTI AL SUGO DI SEPPIE
Linguine or Spaghetti with Squid Sauce

INSALATA DI CAVOLFIORI
Cauliflower Salad

SEMIFREDDO DI RICOTTA ED AMARETTI
Ricotta and Amaretti Mousse

Wine: Soave

———

BACCALÀ MANTECATO
Creamed Salt Cod

PASTA COL CAVOLFIORE BIANCO E NERO
Pasta with White or Purple Cauliflower

INSALATA GIORNALIERA
Everyday Salad

CROSTATA DI MELE AL CROCCANTE
Apple Tart with Croccante

Wine: Gavi

———

MELANZANE IN POTACCHIO
Eggplant with Sauce

PASTA ALLA SARDA
Sardinian Pasta

INSALATA DI ARUGOLA ED INDIVIA BELGA
Arugula and Belgian Endive Salad

SAMOCA AFFOGATO
Drowned Samoca

Wine: Trebbiano d'Abruzzo

PEPERONI ALLA NAPOLETANA
Neapolitan-Style Peppers

PASTA AFFUMICATA
Smoked Pasta

INSALATA TRICOLORE
Tricolored Salad

SPUMA DI LIMONE
Lemon Mousse

Wine: Valpolicella

———

ANTIPASTO ALL'ITALIANA
Italian Antipasto

PENNE AL COCCIO
Pasta in Earthenware

INSALATA DI FAGIOLINI MIMOSA
String Bean Salad Mimosa

IL TARTUFO DI CARMELINA
Carmelina's Ice Cream Truffle

Wine: Amarone

———

COZZE ALLA TARANTINA
Taranto-Style Mussels

FUSILLI ALLA FRANCA FALCONE
Franca Falcone's Fusilli

INSALATA ALLA SICILIANA
Sicilian-Style Salad

TORTA DI MANDORLE
Almond Cake

Wine: Corvo Bianco

SUFFLÉ AL FORMAGGIO
Cheese Soufflé

MACCHERONI ALLA CHITARRA COI FUNGHI
Guitar Macaroni with Mushrooms

INSALATA DI POMODORI E CETRIOLI
Tomato and Cucumber Salad

PERE AL LIQUORE
Pears in Liqueur

Wine: Dolcetto d'Alba

———

SFORMATO DI SPINACI E CARCIOFI
Spinach and Artichoke Flan

BIGOLI IN SALSA D'ACCIUGHE
Whole-Wheat Pasta with Anchovy Sauce

INSALATA VARIEGATA
Streaked Salad

SPUMA DI LIMONE
Lemon Mousse

Wine: Verdicchio

———

TAPENATA ALLA LIGURE
Ligurian Eggplant and Olive Spread

TORTELLINI TARTUFFATI ALLA PANNA
Tortellini with Cream and Truffles

INSALATA GIORNALIERA
Everyday Salad

PERE E FORMAGGIO
Pears and Cheese

Wine: Nebbiolo d'Alba

SCAMPI ALLA BUONGUSTAIA
Shrimps à la Connoisseur

GNOCCHI ALLA GIORDANO
Gnocchi Giordano Style

LA CAPRESE
Capri-Style Salad

CUORICINI ALLA CREMA
Little Hearts in Cream

Wine: Frascati

A PERFECT BIRTHDAY DINNER

SALAME DI TONNO
Tuna Salami

PASTICCIO DI TAGLIATELLE ALLA FINANZIERA
Financier-Style Tagliatelle Timbales

INSALATA SEMPLICE DI FAGIOLINI
Simple String Bean Salad

SPUMA DI LIMONE
Lemon Mousse

Wine: Chianti

Menus for Winter

LA GHIOTTA
The Glutton

RAVIOLI DI RICOTTA
Ricotta-Stuffed Ravioli

INSALATA INVERNALE
Little Winter Salad

TORTA DI AMARETTI
Amaretti Torte

Wine: Brunello di Montalcino

———

TRIPPA ALLA FIORENTINA
Tripe Florentine Style

PASTA CON LE SARDE ALLA PALERMITANA
Palermo-Style Pasta with Sardines

INSALATA VARIEGATA
Streaked Salad

BOCCONOTTI ALL'ABRUZZESE
Little Stuffed Pies

Wine: Vernaccia di San Gimignano

MELANZANE RIPIENE AL FORMAGGIO
Cheese-Stuffed Eggplant

SPAGHETTI DEL POLLAIOLO
Poultry Man's Spaghetti

INSALATA GIORNALIERA
Everyday Salad

BUDINO DI RICOTTA
Ricotta Pudding

Wine: Chianti

━━━

ZUCCHINATA ALLA HODGY-PODGY
Zucchini and Squash Pie

MACCHERONI ALLA NORDICA
Nordic Macaroni

INSALATA DI POMODORI E CETRIOLI
Tomato and Cucumber Salad

ARANCE E KIWI ALL'AMARETTO
Oranges and Kiwis with Amaretto

Wine: Grumello

━━━

FINOCCHI IN PINZIMONIO
Piquant Fennel Antipasto

PENNE ALL'ARRABBIATA
Angry Pasta

INSALATA DI CAVOLI ALLA TORINESE
Turin-Style Cabbage Salad

SORBETTO DI MORTELLE E ANANAS
Cranberry and Pineapple Sherbet

Wine: Inferno

PEPERONI ALLA SARDA
Sardinian Peppers

RIGATONI ALLA BURINA
Bully's Rigatoni

INSALATA VARIEGATA
Streaked Salad

SPUMONE ALL'AURUM
Golden Froth

Wine: Bardolino

SPUMA AL SALMONE
Salmon Mousse

TAGLIATELLE ALLA CAPRESE
Capri-Style Egg Noodles with Vegetables and Vodka

INSALATA VARIEGATA
Streaked Salad

SORBETTO ALLO SPUMANTE
Champagne Sherbet

Wine: Prosecco di Conegliano

CROSTINI MIEI
My Crostini

TROCCOLI ALLA DAUNIA
Thick Square Noodles Daunia Style

TAPENATA LIGURE IN INSALATA
Ligurian Tapenata in a Salad

PIZZA DOLCE ALL'ARANCIA E CIOCCOLATA
Orange and Chocolate Cake

Wine: Aglianico del Vulture

BACCALÀ ALLA VICENTINA
Salt Cod Vicenza Style

SPAGHETTI CON LE COZZE ALLA NAPOLETANA
Spaghetti with Mussels Neapolitan Style

INSALATA TRICOLORE
Tricolored Salad

CREMOLATA AL CAFFE
Coffee Pudding

Wine: Greco di Tufo

———

MOZZARELLA IN CARROZZA CON ACCIUGHE
Fried Mozzarella and Anchovy Sandwiches

CHICCHE VERDI DEL NONNO
Grandpa's Green Dumplings

INSALATA CAPRICCIOSA
Capricious Salad

SORBETTO ALLO SPUMANTE
Champagne Sherbet

Wine: Spanna

———

TOTANI RIPIENI
Stuffed Squid

CAVATELLI CON L'ARUGOLA
Little Dumplings with Arugula

INSALATA RUSSA
Russian Salad

MELE ALL'ANTICA
Antique-Style Apples

Wine: Orvieto

TRADITIONAL DISHES FOR CHRISTMAS

ANTIPASTO ALL'ITALIANA
Italian Antipasto

TIMBALLO DI MACCHERONI ALLA NONNINA
Grandmother's Macaroni Timbale

GIARDINIERA
Garden Salad

CASSATA ALLA SULMONESE
Sulmona-Style Cassata

Wine: Chianti Classico

———

TEGAMINO ALLA MIMI
Mimi's Little Casserole

LASAGNE VERDI ALLA MODENESE
Modena-Style Green Lasagna

INSALATINA INVERNALE
Little Winter Salad

PARROZZO DI PAPÀ
Papa's Rough Christmas Bread

Wine: Vino Nobile di Montepulciano

NEW YEAR'S EVE SUPPER

COTECHINO DELLA VIGILIA DI CAPODANNO
New Year's Eve Cotechino

TORTELLINI CON LA SALSA DI FEGATO D'OCA
Tortellini in Goose Liver Sauce

INSALATA DELLA VIGILIA DI CAPODANNO
New Year's Eve Salad

SORBETTO ALLO SPUMANTE
Champagne Sherbet

Wines: Brusco dei Barbi
Prosecco di Valdobbiadene

THE
RECIPES

Appetizers

6 slices prosciutto
6 slices salami
6 slices mortadella
6 slices ham
¹/₄ pound mozzarella cheese, cut into strips
1 jar (6 ounces) marinated artichokes, drained and
  halved
6 anchovy fillets, rolled into coils
12 green or black olives
3 hard-cooked eggs, cut into wedges
Parsley sprigs, for garnish

ANTIPASTO ALL'ITALIANA
Italian Antipasto
Serves 6

Place all of the meats on a serving platter, alternating the different types in a decorative fashion. Add the mozzarella strips and arrange decoratively. Place the artichokes in the center and spot the anchovies all around. Scatter the olives over the platter. Place the egg wedges around the artichokes, like the petals of a flower, or all around the border of the platter. Decorate with sprigs of parsley and serve.

PANE E SALAME
Bread and Salami
Serves 6

This is a delicious antipasto with almost any meal—especially when soup is included. You will see your guests really enjoy this simple repast, so do not serve too much of it and don't slice the entire salami; let them do the work. It will curb their enthusiasm a little, especially if the salami is one of those hard chewy little devils.

1 loaf crusty Italian bread, sliced on the bias
1 Italian salami such as *cacciatore*, Sicilian, Abruzzese, *sopressata*, or *capocollo*

1. Arrange the slices of bread on one end of a cutting board. Place a skinned salami and a knife in front of the bread.
2. Cut only a few slices and let the guests slice the remainder at will.

POMODORI ALL'ADRIATICA
Tomatoes Adriatic
Serves 6

6 medium tomatoes
Salt
1 pound cooked fresh fish, such as cod, haddock, or sole
¹/₄ pound cooked shrimp
2 tablespoons olive oil
¹/₂ teaspoon prepared mustard
2 tablespoons mayonnaise
Fresh lemon juice to taste
1 tablespoon minced capers
1 tablespoon minced fresh parsley

1. Cut off the tomato tops, scoop out the pulp, and chop it. Squeeze the tomato shells gently to remove the seeds and liquid. Sprinkle with salt and turn upside down to drain.
2. Flake the fish. Reserve 6 shrimp for decoration and coarsely chop the remaining shrimp.
3. In a bowl, combine the oil with all the remaining ingredients. Add the chopped tomato pulp, fish, and chopped shrimp and mix well.
4. Fill the tomato shells with the mixture and decorate each tomato with one of the reserved shrimp. Chill before serving.

This is a simple antipasto. The fennel (*finocchi*) wedges are dipped into an oil-and-pepper combination called *pinzimonio*, which means piquant or hot.

FINOCCHI IN PINZIMONIO
Piquant Fennel Antipasto
Serves 6

2 large fennel bulbs
³/₄ cup virgin olive oil
2 garlic cloves, minced
Juice of 1 lemon
Freshly ground pepper

1. Wash and trim the fennel. Cut into thin wedges and place in a serving basket or bowl.
2. In a bowl, combine the oil, garlic, lemon juice, and quite a bit of pepper. Whisk and pour into a little bowl for dipping.

NOTE: You will have quite a bit of oil left. Use it for salads or cooking, if pepper doesn't intrude on the recipe.

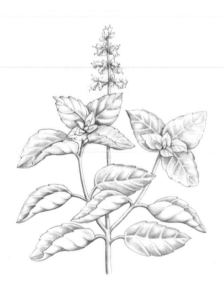

CIAMBOTTA ALLA FEDERICO SPERA
Fried Vegetables Federico Spera
Serves 6

This is my cousin Federico's recipe. No matter how good I make it, he will always say that his *ciambotta* is the best.

6 tablespoons oil
1 garlic clove
1 onion, sliced
2 peppers, sliced
1 medium-sized eggplant, cubed
2 zucchini, cut into bite-sized pieces
1 cauliflower head, cut into florets
4 tablespoons fine bread crumbs
Salt and freshly ground pepper to taste
1 tablespoon chopped fresh basil or oregano
1 tablespoon minced fresh parsley

1. Place oil and garlic in a skillet and heat until the garlic starts to fry. Stir-fry each vegetable separately until it is just tender (this is the secret of the success of this recipe). Set aside.
2. When you have fried each vegetable separately, return all of them to the skillet and heat through. Sprinkle with bread crumbs, salt and pepper, basil or oregano, and parsley. Serve warm.

ANTIPASTO DI CAVOLFIORE
Cauliflower Florets and Dip
Serves 6

1 large cauliflower
1 cup mayonnaise (see page 41)
1 tablespoon grainy mustard
1 tablespoon minced fresh parsley

1. Break the cauliflower into florets and cut the stems into sticks. Chill.
2. Arrange the cauliflower in a basket or on a serving platter. Place the mayonnaise in a small bowl; stir in the grainy mustard and parsley. Fit the bowl into the center of the florets and serve chilled.

PEPERONI ALLA NAPOLETANA
Neapolitan-Style Peppers
Serves 6

6 large green, red, or yellow bell peppers or a mixture of
  the three
¼ cup olive oil
1 tablespoon minced fresh parsley
1 tablespoon capers
Salt and freshly ground pepper
20 black olives, pitted and sliced
4 tablespoons fine dry bread crumbs
3 to 4 anchovy fillets, chopped

1. Roast the peppers directly on a gas flame or directly under an electric broiler. Turn often until the skin is charred. Drop the peppers into a brown bag, close, and let steam for 10 minutes. (This will make the peeling easier.) Cool, peel, and core the peppers; cut them into julienne strips.
2. In a bowl, combine the peppers with the oil, parsley, capers, and salt and pepper to taste. Add the olives and toss.
3. Preheat the oven to 375°. Oil a 9-inch pie pan and sprinkle with 2 tablespoons of the bread crumbs; discard the excess crumbs. Place half of the pepper mixture in one layer in the prepared pan. Scatter the anchovies all over and add the remaining pepper mixture. Smooth the top and sprinkle with the remaining 2 tablespoons bread crumbs. Bake for 15 minutes, until hot.

NOTE: This dish is also excellent when served at room temperature.

PEPERONI ALLA SARDA
Sardinian Peppers
Serves 6

About 1/2 cup olive oil
6 large red or green bell peppers
4 garlic cloves
1 can (2 ounces) anchovy fillets, chopped
1 cup fresh bread crumbs
2 cans (7 ounces each) tunafish, drained and flaked
1 cup peeled, seeded, and chopped tomatoes, or use canned tomatoes, drained and chopped
2 tablespoons capers, drained
5 to 6 parsley sprigs, chopped
Pinch of basil
1/4 cup pine nuts (optional)

1. Preheat the oven to 375°. Lightly oil a baking dish in which peppers will stand snugly. Stem, core, and seed the peppers.
2. In a large skillet, warm 1/2 cup oil over moderate heat. Add the garlic and sauté. As soon as the garlic starts to fry, add the anchovies and bread crumbs and sauté, stirring, for a few minutes. Remove the garlic and discard it.
3. Add the tuna, tomatoes, capers, parsley, basil, and pine nuts, if desired, and cook, stirring, for 5 minutes. Fill the peppers with the mixture and stand them in the prepared pan. Drizzle a little additional olive oil over each pepper and bake, uncovered, until tender, about 1 hour.

TEGAMINO ALLA MIMI
Mimi's Little Casserole
Serves 6

This is one of my favorite recipes. I re-created it after eating it at one of my favorite New York restaurants, Salta in Bocca.

3 red bell peppers, roasted, skinned, seeded, and cut in half
6 anchovy fillets
6 slices mozzarella cheese

1. Preheat the oven to 375°. Place the pepper halves on a cookie sheet or in individual ovenproof dishes. Top each half with an anchovy fillet and one slice of the mozzarella.
2. Bake for 15 to 20 minutes, until the cheese melts. Serve at once.

24 asparagus spears, blanched
Olive oil
Juice of 1 lemon
6 thin slices boiled ham
Watercress or fresh parsley sprigs, for garnish

ASPARAGI AL PROSCIUTTO COTTO
Ham-Wrapped Asparagus
Serves 6

1. Cut each asparagus spear into a 6-inch length. Reserve the tough stems for another use.
2. In a bowl, dress the asparagus with the oil and lemon juice and chill.
3. Before serving, wrap 4 of the asparagus spears in one slice of the ham and set on a salad plate. Wrap the remaining spears in the same fashion. Decorate the plates with watercress or parsley and serve.

6 small zucchini
Oil for frying
2 tablespoons chopped fresh mint
2 to 3 garlic cloves, minced
Salt
¹/₄ cup red wine vinegar

ZUCCHINE A SCAPECE
Marinated Zucchini
Serves 6

1. Cut the zucchini into thin slices and spread them on a cloth to dry for 1 hour.
2. In a deep fryer, with very hot oil that is almost smoking, fry the zucchini in small batches until golden brown on both sides. Drain on paper towels and layer the slices in a terrine or bowl. Continue until all the zucchini are fried, drained, and layered.
3. Sprinkle the mint, garlic, and salt over the terrine and pour on the vinegar. Cover and set aside for at least 1 hour or overnight.

NOTE: Zucchini prepared this way are better the next day.

ZUCCHINATA ALLA HODGY-PODGY
Zucchini and Squash Pie
Serves 6

My husband, Harold, named this recipe when it was invented on a hot summer day while we were busy packing for our long-awaited Italian vacation. It was lunchtime and we were hungry, with only two zucchini, one green and one yellow, in the house. This dish is what resulted from the zucchini and a bit of rummaging in the refrigerator. I have extended the recipe to serve six.

3 tablespoons olive oil
1 garlic clove
1 to 2 fresh basil leaves
3 zucchini, thinly sliced
3 yellow summer squash, thinly sliced
Butter for pie plate
Freshly grated Parmesan cheese
1 to 2 slices prosciutto or bacon, shredded
3/4 cup cooked tomato or meat sauce
2 eggs beaten with 2 tablespoons milk

1. In a large skillet, preferably nonstick, warm the oil over moderate heat. Add the garlic, basil, and zucchini and sauté until just softened. Remove the zucchini with tongs or a slotted spoon and drain on paper towels. Sauté the yellow squash in the same way and drain on paper towels (you might need to add a bit more oil).
2. Preheat the oven to 375°. Butter a 9-inch pie plate from which you can serve. Arrange a layer of zucchini or squash on the bottom of the pie plate. Sprinkle with a good handful of Parmesan and half of the prosciutto. Top with half of the sauce.
3. Alternating zucchini and squash slices, stand the slices on edge to make a rim all around the edge of the pie plate, creating a scalloped edge for the pie.
4. Continue layering the vegetables as before, finishing with a final layer of vegetables. Sprinkle the top with a handful of Parmesan and pour the egg-milk mixture over the top. Bake until the eggs are set and top is nicely golden, 15 to 20 minutes.

This dish is a version of a typical Abruzzese recipe re-created by my young niece, Marcella Vita-Colonna.

LA GHIOTTA
The Glutton
Serves 8

1 carrot
1 celery rib
2 to 3 parsley sprigs
1 garlic clove
3 zucchini, sliced
3 red or green bell peppers, seeded and sliced
3 medium potatoes, peeled and sliced
3 onions, sliced into rings
Olive oil
Oregano
Salt and freshly ground pepper

1. Preheat the oven to 350°. In a food processor or blender, combine the carrot, celery, parsley, and garlic. Process to chop finely.
2. Generously oil a baking/serving dish and alternately layer the sliced vegetables, sprinkling each layer with the chopped vegetable mixture.
3. Drizzle generously with olive oil and sprinkle with oregano and salt and pepper to taste. Bake until the vegetables are tender, 45 minutes to 1 hour. Pour off the excess oil, cool, and serve.

CROSTINI MIEI
My Crostini
Serves 8

3 tablespoons olive oil
1 garlic clove, peeled
1 small onion, thinly sliced
3 tablespoons sherry or Marsala wine
1 tablespoon dried *porcini* mushrooms, soaked in $1/2$ cup warm water
$3/4$ pound fresh mushrooms
1 tablespoon capers
1 teaspoon anchovy paste (optional)
1 tablespoon minced fresh parsley
1 loaf Italian bread, thinly sliced

1. In a large skillet, combine the oil, garlic, and onion. Cook, stirring, over moderate heat for a few minutes. Add the sherry or Marsala.

2. Remove the *porcini* from their soaking water and set aside. Strain the liquid through a double thickness of dampened cheesecloth and add to the pan. Cover and cook over low heat for 10 minutes.

3. Add the dried and fresh mushrooms and cook over moderate heat until the mushrooms give up their liquid and it has been absorbed.

4. Preheat the oven to 375°. Stir in the capers and anchovy paste and remove from the heat.

5. Transfer the mixture to a food processor or blender and add half of the parsley. Chop until smooth. Spread the mixture on the bread slices and bake the *crostini* for 15 minutes. Serve hot, sprinkled with the remaining parsley.

SFORMATO DI SPINACI E CARCIOFI
Spinach and Artichoke Flan
Serves 6 to 8

3 tablespoons unsalted butter
1 medium onion, chopped
1 package (9 ounces) frozen artichoke hearts, thawed, or 10 to 12 very small fresh artichokes, trimmed and quartered
2½ pounds fresh spinach, washed and coarsely chopped
Pinch of tarragon
Pinch of marjoram
½ cup fine dry bread crumbs
¾ cup shredded smoked mozzarella cheese
2 eggs, lightly beaten

1. Preheat the oven to 350°. Butter a pie pan. In a large skillet, melt the butter over moderate heat. Add the onion and cook until tender, about 5 minutes. Add the artichoke hearts and cover. Reduce heat to low and cook until tender. Add a bit of water if necessary. Frozen artichokes will need very little cooking.

2. Add the spinach and cook, tossing, until wilted. Turn the mixture into a mixing bowl and add the tarragon, marjoram, bread crumbs, mozzarella, and eggs. Mix well and turn into the prepared pan. Smooth the top and bake for 25 minute, until set.

1 pound small fresh mushrooms
1/4 cup olive oil
1 garlic clove
2 parsley sprigs, minced
Freshly ground pepper
1/4 cup dry white wine
Lemon juice
1 tablespoon red wine vinegar
1 bay leaf
1 clove

FUNGHETTI MARINATI
Marinated Mushrooms
Serves 6

1. Remove the stems from the mushrooms and reserve for another use.
2. In a large skillet, warm the oil over moderate heat. Add the garlic, mushrooms, and half of the parsley. Stir-fry for 3 minutes. Add pepper to taste, along with the wine, lemon juice to taste, vinegar, bay leaf, and clove. Cover and cook for 10 minutes. Cool to room temperature and refrigerate in a closed jar.

NOTE: These mushrooms should be done at least a day before you want to serve them. They will keep for a week.

18 medium mushrooms
Lemon juice
2 garlic cloves
2 to 3 parsley sprigs
1 tablespoon capers
2 to 3 tablespoons fresh bread crumbs
1 to 2 teaspoons olive oil

FUNGHI RIPIENI AI CAPPERI
Stuffed Mushrooms with Capers
Serves 6

1. Preheat the oven to 375°. Wipe the mushrooms with a damp cloth. Remove the stems and reserve. Sprinkle the caps with lemon juice and set aside.
2. In a food processor or blender, combine the mushroom stems, garlic, parsley, and capers and chop very fine. Add the bread crumbs and just enough of the oil to moisten the mixture. Process for a few seconds, until blended.
3. Fill the caps with the stuffing mixture. Place the caps, stuffing side up, on oiled baking sheets and bake until heated through, 20 to 30 minutes.

FUNGHI FARCITI AL PROSCIUTTO COTTO E SALAME
Stuffed Mushrooms with Ham and Salami
Serves 6 to 8

I once saw the restaurateur Alfredo Viazzi make a similar recipe. I have re-created it from memory, and I hope to the satisfaction of the original creator.

36 large fresh mushrooms
4 thick slices Genoa salami, coarsely chopped
8 thin slices prosciutto or ham, coarsely chopped
2 tablespoons finely minced parsley
Pinch each of thyme, oregano, and sage
Freshly ground pepper
$1/2$ cup freshly grated Parmesan cheese
$2/3$ cup chicken stock

1. Preheat the oven to 375°. Carefully remove the stems from the mushrooms and set aside.
2. In a food processor, finely chop the mushroom stems. With the machine running, add the salami, prosciutto or ham, parsley, herbs, pepper to taste, and $1/4$ cup of the Parmesan. Process until finely chopped.
3. Stuff the mushroom caps with the mixture. Pour the chicken stock into a square baking pan and arrange the filled mushrooms in it, stuffing side up. Bake until heated through, 20 to 25 minutes. Increase the oven temperature to broil.
4. Sprinkle the remaining $1/4$ cup Parmesan over the mushrooms and broil for 3 minutes. Remove the mushrooms to a serving dish. Reserve any remaining stock for another use or discard it. Serve the stuffed mushrooms at once.

CROSTONI AI FUNGHI
Mushroom Toast
Serves 6 to 8

2 tablespoons unsalted butter
1 small onion, thinly sliced
2 to 3 tablespoons dry white wine
2 pounds fresh mushrooms, thinly sliced
Salt and freshly ground pepper
8 slices crusty bread
8 thin slices Fontina cheese
2 parsley sprigs, minced

1. Preheat the oven to 375°. In a skillet, melt the butter over low heat. Add the onion and cook until the onion starts to color, 5 to 7 minutes. Add the wine and let it evaporate, about 3 minutes. Add the mushrooms and season with salt and pepper to taste. Cover the skillet and cook over moderately low heat for 30 minutes.

2. Meanwhile, trim the bread and Fontina slices to equal size. Place a slice of the cheese on each slice of bread. Place the bread and cheese on a baking sheet and bake until the cheese starts to melt, about 5 minutes.

3. Top the slices of bread with some of the mushroom mixture and sprinkle with the parsley. Serve at once.

TAPENATA ALLA LIGURE
Ligurian Tuna and Olive Spread

1 can (7 ounces) Italian oil-packed tunafish
Up to $1/2$ cup olive oil
2 to 3 garlic cloves, minced
3 parsley sprigs
4 to 5 basil leaves
12 pitted black olives
3 tablespoons capers
Juice of 1 lemon
Olives, for garnish

1. Drain the tuna oil into a measuring cup. Add olive oil to measure $1/2$ cup. In a food processor or blender, combine all of the ingredients except the garnish. Process to a fine purée and turn into a bowl; chill.

2. Pour the mixture into a serving dish and garnish with the olives. Serve with crusty bread, crackers, or pita bread.

NOTE: This can be served as a dip for crudités.

CAPONATA ALLA SICILIANA CON SALSA SAN BERNARDO

Sicilian Caponata with San Bernardo Sauce

Serves 8

This is the classic Sicilian recipe. Its sauce, with a touch of chocolate, is unique.

½ cup vegetable oil
3 medium eggplants, peeled and cubed
5 to 6 celery ribs, tender part only, cut into 1-inch-long julienne
2 tablespoons olive oil
1 onion, chopped
⅓ cup red wine vinegar
1 tablespoon sugar
¾ cup tomato sauce or purée
2 tablespoons capers, drained
1 cup Sicilian olives, pitted
2 tablespoons minced fresh parsley
Salsa San Bernardo
Hard-cooked eggs, for garnish (optional)

1. In a large skillet, warm the vegetable oil over moderate heat until almost smoking. Add the eggplant and sauté until nicely colored, about 10 minutes. You may need more oil. With a slotted spoon, remove the eggplant to a bowl and set aside. Add the celery to the skillet and sauté until tender. Remove with a slotted spoon and set aside.

2. In a heatproof casserole, warm the olive oil over moderate heat. Add the onion and cook over low heat until soft and translucent, 5 to 7 minutes. Add the vinegar, sugar, and tomato sauce and mix well. Simmer for 10 minutes. Add the capers, olives, parsley, and the reserved eggplant and celery. Mix and simmer until heated through, 5 to 10 minutes.

3. To serve, turn the *caponata* onto a round serving dish and mound it in the middle. Allow to cool. Cover with the Sauce San Bernardo and smooth with a spatula. Decorate with hard-cooked eggs, if desired.

SALSA SAN BERNARDO

1 tablespoon olive oil
1 cup blanched almonds
2 to 3 slices toasted bread, torn into bits
1 teaspoon anchovy paste

1 tablespoon coarsely chopped unsweetened chocolate
Juice of 1 orange
1 scant tablespoon sugar
¹/₄ cup red wine vinegar

1. In a small skillet, warm the oil over moderate heat. Sauté the almonds, stirring often, until lightly colored, about 5 minutes.
2. In a food processor or blender, combine the almonds, bread, anchovy paste, and chocolate. Process to form a paste.
3. Turn the paste into a small saucepan. Add the orange juice, sugar, vinegar, and about 2 tablespoons of water. The mixture will be quite loose; if not, add a bit more water. Cook, stirring, over low heat until the sauce is dense and smooth.

TAPENATA LIGURE IN INSALATA
Ligurian Tapenade in a Salad
Serves 8

2 cans (7 ounces each) Italian oil-packed tunafish
Olive oil
2 to 3 garlic cloves, minced
3 parsley sprigs
4 to 5 basil leaves
20 pitted black olives
3 tablespoons capers, drained
Juice of 1 lemon
Olives, for garnish
2 heads Belgian endive
1 head radicchio

1. Drain the tuna into a measuring cup. Add olive oil, if necessary, to measure ¹/₂ cup. In a food processor or blender, combine the oil, garlic, parsley, basil, olives, capers, lemon juice, and tuna. Purée until smooth. Cover and chill.
2. Pour the mixture into a shallow serving bowl and decorate the top with the olives. Insert the leaves of the endive and radicchio around the edges of the bowl, either alternately or in a double row, one row of endive, one row of radicchio.

NOTE: If radicchio is not available, use bronze lettuce.

MELANZANE IN POTACCHIO
Eggplant with Sauce
Serves 6 to 8

¼ cup olive oil
1 garlic clove
1 large onion, sliced
2 medium eggplants, cubed
1 can (16 ounces) peeled Italian plum tomatoes or tomato purée
Pinch of oregano
Salt and freshly ground pepper

1. In a large skillet, warm the oil over moderate heat. Add the garlic and onion and cook until onion is translucent, 5 to 7 minutes. Add eggplant and cook, stirring, for a few minutes. Stir in the tomatoes, oregano, and salt and pepper to taste. Cover and cook until the eggplant is cooked, 35 to 40 minutes.
2. Serve hot with garlic bread.

NOTE: You can add some Italian or bell peppers with the onion if you wish, and proceed as described.

MELANZANE RIPIENE AL FORMAGGIO
Cheese-Stuffed Eggplant
Serves 8

4 medium eggplants
About 6 tablespoons olive oil
2 medium onions, chopped
2 garlic cloves, minced
4 plum tomatoes, peeled, seeded, and coarsely chopped
1 tablespoon tomato paste
Pinch of oregano
¾ cup unflavored dry bread crumbs
8 ounces mozzarella cheese, shredded
2 to 3 parsley sprigs, minced
2 small potatoes, boiled and diced
4 eggs, beaten
Salt and freshly ground pepper
Grated Pecorino Romano cheese

1. Preheat oven to 375°. Cut the eggplants lengthwise in half. Brush each half with a little oil and bake for 20 minutes. Scoop out the pulp and chop coarsely. Reserve the shells and set aside.

2. In a large skillet, warm 4 tablespoons of the oil over moderate heat. Add the onions and cook until soft and translucent. Add the garlic and reserved eggplant pulp and sauté for about 3 minutes, adding more oil if necessary. Stir in the tomatoes. Dissolve the tomato paste in ¼ cup water and stir into the eggplant mixture. Cook until the water is absorbed, 5 to 6 minutes. Add the oregano.

3. Remove from heat. Add the bread crumbs, mozzarella, parsley, potatoes, eggs, and salt and pepper to taste. Fill the eggplant shells with the mixture and smooth the top. Sprinkle with the Romano cheese.

4. Oil a baking pan that will hold the eggplants in one layer. Bake until the eggplant shells are tender, about 45 minutes.

ANTIPASTO DI MOZZARELLA ALL'ERBETTE
Mozzarella Antipasto with Herbs
Serves 6

1 pound mozzarella cheese, sliced
¼ cup plus 1 tablespoon olive oil
1 tablespoon chopped fresh parsley
2 anchovy fillets, mashed
1 tablespoon freshly grated Parmesan or Pecorino cheese
1 tablespoon chopped capers
Pinch of oregano
Pane casareccio (homemade bread)

1. Arrange the slices of mozzarella in one layer on a serving dish.
2. In a small bowl, combine all of the remaining ingredients except the bread. Mix well and pour over the mozzarella. Chill for about 1 hour. Serve at room temperature with *pane casareccio*.

MOZZARELLA IN CARROZZA CON ACCIUGHE
Fried Mozzarella and Anchovy Sandwiches
Serves 6

1 loaf (1 pound) sliced sandwich bread
1¹/₂ pounds mozzarella cheese
1 can (2 ounces) anchovy fillets
Oil, for deep frying
All-purpose flour
3 eggs beaten with 2 to 3 tablespoons milk

1. Cut the bread slices diagonally in half. Cut the mozzarella into 12 slices, matching the shape and size of the bread slices as much as possible. Sandwich a slice of mozzarella and a small piece of anchovy between each two slices of bread. Insert a toothpick to keep the slices together.
2. Meanwhile, heat about 1 inch of the oil to the smoking point. Set the flour on a shallow dish and dredge the sandwiches in it. Dip each sandwich into the egg-milk mixture.
3. Fry 2 to 3 sandwiches at a time until golden brown on both sides. Drain on paper towels and serve hot.

SUFFLÉ AL FORMAGGIO
Cheese Soufflé
Serves 6

4¹/₂ tablespoons unsalted butter
1¹/₂ cups plus 1 tablespoon grated Parmesan and Gruyère
  cheeses, mixed together
4¹/₂ tablespoons all-purpose flour
1¹/₂ cups milk
Pinch of salt
Pinch of pepper
Pinch of freshly grated nutmeg
6 egg yolks, at room temperature
7 egg whites, at room temperature
¹/₈ teaspoon cream of tartar

1. Preheat the oven to 400°. Rub ¹/₂ tablespoon of the butter over the bottom and sides of a 1¹/₂-quart soufflé dish. Sprinkle the dish with 1 tablespoon of the grated cheeses. Butter a strip of foil or parchment and tie it around the dish to form a 3-inch collar.

2. In a heavy saucepan, melt the remaining 4 tablespoons butter over moderate heat. Add the flour and cook over low heat until well blended. Remove from the heat and add the milk, a little at a time, stirring constantly until the mixture is smooth and liquid. Return the saucepan to the heat and cook the sauce over low heat until it starts to boil. Off heat, add the salt, pepper, and nutmeg. One at a time, add the egg yolks, beating well after each addition. Add the remaining 1 1/2 cups grated cheese and mix well.

3. In a bowl, beat the egg whites with the cream of tartar until foamy. Continue beating until peaks form and the mixture is stiff but not dry.

4. Gently but thoroughly, fold the egg whites into the cheese mixture. Pour the mixture into the prepared dish.

5. Place the dish on the bottom shelf of the oven and reduce the heat to 375°. Bake for 30 minutes for a soufflé with a runny center. For a well-cooked soufflé, reduce the oven temperature to 325° and bake for 45 minutes. Serve immediately.

---

6 hard-cooked eggs
3 tablespoons olive oil
1 to 2 tablespoons caviar
2 tablespoons chopped fresh parsley
1 tablespoon chopped onion or scallions
Juice of 1 lemon
Lettuce
Radishes, tomato slices, and scallions, for garnish

UOVA AL CAVIALE
Eggs with Caviar
Serves 6

1. Halve the eggs and remove the egg yolks to a bowl. Add the oil and mash together. Add the caviar, parsley, onion or scallions, and lemon juice; mix well.

2. Taste the mixture; if too salty (this depends on the caviar), add additional lemon juice. Stuff the egg whites with the mixture and chill.

3. Serve the eggs on a bed of lettuce, garnished with radishes, tomato slices, and scallions.

UOVA DELICATE
Melt-in-the-Mouth Eggs
Serves 6

6 hard-cooked eggs, peeled
3 tablespoons Béchamel Sauce (see page 42)
3 tablespoons freshly grated Parmesan cheese
Pinch of freshly grated nutmeg
Salt and freshly ground pepper
1/2 cup all-purpose flour
1 egg, beaten
Fine dry bread crumbs
2 cups peanut oil, for frying

1. Halve the eggs lengthwise and remove the yolks. In a bowl, mash the yolks and add the béchamel, Parmesan, nutmeg, and salt and pepper to taste; mix well.
2. Mound a generous amount of the yolk mixture into the depression of one egg half and top with the other half of the egg. Stuff the remaining 5 eggs in the same manner.
3. Place the flour on a shallow plate, the beaten egg in a shallow bowl, and the bread crumbs on a third dish. Roll each stuffed egg first in the flour, then in the egg, and finally in the bread crumbs. Refrigerate for at least 30 minutes. (The recipe can be done to this point ahead of time.)
4. In a deep fryer, heat the oil to the smoking point. Deep-fry all of the eggs at once, turning frequently, until golden brown on all sides, 5 to 10 minutes. Serve hot.

NOTE: These eggs may be served, halved, as finger food if you prefer. They also reheat quite well in a 350° oven.

More than a fancy omelet but easier to make. All you need is a touch of fantasy and vegetables to mix and match at your pleasure.

2 tablespoons olive oil
1/2 package frozen artichoke hearts, thawed and halved
1 garlic clove, minced
1/2 package frozen peas, thawed
Salt and freshly ground pepper
1 tablespoon minced fresh parsley
1 tablespoon all-purpose flour
2 tablespoons freshly grated Parmesan cheese
2 tablespoons milk
6 eggs, well beaten
2 tablespoons unsalted butter

1. Preheat the oven to 350°. In a heavy iron or other ovenproof skillet, warm the oil over moderate heat. Add the artichokes and garlic and cook for 5 minutes, shaking the pan to prevent sticking. Add the peas and cook for 5 more minutes. Season to taste with salt and pepper. Add the parsley, stir, cover, and reduce the heat to low.

2. In a bowl, mix the flour, Parmesan, and milk. Add the beaten eggs and mix to blend. Pour the vegetables into the egg mixture and mix well.

3. Wipe out the skillet with paper towels and melt the butter in it. Pour in the vegetable-egg mixture and cook over moderate heat until the bottom sets, about 5 minutes.

4. Place the skillet in the oven and bake until the top is golden brown, about 30 minutes.

5. Turn the *tortino* onto a serving dish, if you wish, and slice.

NOTE: Other suggestions for *tortini*: *tortino* with zucchini and onions; with carrots and peas; with cardoons (an edible Mediterranean plant related to the artichoke, available at many greengrocers) and eggs. They are all made the same way. The seasoning can be changed according to your taste.

SPUMA AL SALMONE
Salmon Mousse
Serves 8 as an antipasto or 12 to 16 as an appetizer with drinks

1 small onion, quartered
5 to 6 parsley sprigs
2 envelopes (¼ ounce each) unflavored gelatin
1 cup hot chicken broth or bouillon
1 can (7 ounces) salmon, drained and picked over
½ cup mayonnaise (see page 41)
2 tablespoons lemon juice
Freshly ground pepper
1 cup heavy cream
Oil, for the mold

1. In a food processor or blender, combine the onion and parsley and process until minced. Do not remove.
2. In a small bowl, dissolve the gelatin in the hot broth. Pour into a food processor or blender, add the salmon, and process until smooth. Add the mayonnaise, lemon juice, and pepper to taste. Process, adding the cream in a steady stream.
3. Lightly oil a fish mold or a 4-cup mold. Fill the mold with the mousse and refrigerate 4 to 5 hours or overnight.
4. To serve, dip the mold into hot water for a few seconds. Unmold and decorate with your favorite garnish.

TORTA DEL PESCATORE
Fisherman's Pie
Serves 6 to 8

3 tablespoons unsalted butter
¼ cup dry bread crumbs
1 pound fresh salmon, bluefish, tuna, or a similar type of fish
1 medium potato, boiled and peeled
¼ pound bacon, chopped
Pinch of sage
2 eggs, lightly beaten
Salt and freshly ground pepper
Milk

1. Preheat the oven to 375°. Butter a 9-inch pie plate from which you can serve. Sprinkle with some of the bread crumbs.
2. Poach or pan-fry the fish. Discard the skin and bones; flake the fish.
3. In a mixing bowl, mash the potato. Add the fish, bacon, remaining bread crumbs, sage, eggs, and salt and pepper to taste.

Add just enough milk to moisten and bind the ingredients well. Pour the mixture into the prepared pie plate and smooth the top. Dot generously with the remaining butter.

4. Bake for about 40 minutes, until set. Serve hot, cut into wedges.

NOTE: Making this torte is a good way to use up leftover fish.

PESCE ALLE OLIVE E CAPPERI
Fish with Olives and Capers
Serves 6

SAUCE

3 tablespoons olive oil
1½ cups tomato purée
1 parsley sprig
Pinch of basil
1 garlic clove
A few flakes of *diavoletto* (Italian hot red pepper flakes, optional)

FISH

All-purpose flour
Salt and freshly ground pepper
6 small red snapper or whiting fillets (about 2 pounds)
3 tablespoons unsalted butter
3 tablespoons olive oil
¼ cup dry white wine
2 tablespoons capers, drained
20 ripe olives, pitted and sliced

1. Make the sauce: In a saucepan, combine all of the ingredients for the sauce. Bring to a boil over moderately high heat, reduce the heat to low, and simmer, uncovered, for 15 minutes. Discard the parsley and garlic and set the sauce aside.

2. Prepare the fish: In a shallow plate, combine the flour and salt and pepper to taste. Dredge the fillets in the seasoned flour and shake off the excess.

3. In one or two skillets, melt the butter with the oil over moderate heat. Add the fillets and sauté for 1 to 2 minutes on each side. Add the wine and cook until it evaporates. Add the sauce and cook for 10 minutes. Stir in the capers and olives and cook until just heated through. Serve at once.

AVOCADO AL TONNO
Avocado with Tunafish
Serves 6

3 ripe avocados
Juice of 1 lemon
1 hard-cooked egg, quartered
1 can (7 ounces) tunafish, drained
1 small pickle, minced
Chopped fresh parsley, for garnish

1. Divide the avocados in half and discard the pits. Sprinkle the flesh with some of the lemon juice to prevent discoloration.
2. In a food processor, combine the egg, tuna, and pickle. Process until smooth. Season with lemon juice to taste.
3. Fill the avocado halves with the tuna mixture and serve, sprinkled with the parsley.

SALAME DI TONNO
Tuna Salami
Serves 6

1 can Italian oil-packed tunafish, drained
1 small potato, boiled and peeled
3 tablespoons fine dry bread crumbs
2 tablespoons freshly grated Parmesan cheese
1 whole egg plug 1 egg white

1. In a mixing bowl, mash together the tuna and potato. Add the bread crumbs, Parmesan, egg, and egg white. Mix well. Wet your hands, and shape the mixture into the form of a salami.
2. Wet a length of cheesecloth, wring it out well, and wrap it around the formed salami. Secure the ends with strings and place the salami in a casserole or Dutch oven. Add water to cover and bring to a boil. Reduce the heat to low and simmer for about 1 hour.
3. Remove the salami from the water and untie it. Discard the cheesecloth, wrap in plastic or foil, and chill.
4. To serve, cut the salami in slices. Arrange on a serving dish and serve with homemade mayonnaise (see page 41), if desired.

1 boneless veal roast (about 3 pounds)
1 can (7 ounces) Italian oil-packed tunafish
2 anchovy fillets, chopped
1 medium onion, sliced
1½ cups red wine
2 *cornichons* or ½ sour pickle
¼ cup mayonnaise
1 tablespoon capers
1 lemon, very thinly sliced, for garnish

VITELLO TONNATO
Tunnied Veal
Serves 6 to 8

1. In a casserole, combine the veal, tunafish, anchovies, onion, and wine over moderate heat. Bring to a boil, reduce the heat to low, and simmer for about 1½ hours, until the meat is tender. Set aside to cool in its own juice.
2. Remove the meat from the casserole and slice very thin. Arrange the slices on a serving dish.
3. Pour the sauce from the casserole into a food processor and add the *cornichons* or pickle. Purée until smooth. Mix with the mayonnaise and pour over the sliced meat.
4. Sprinkle the meat with the capers. Decorate with the lemon slices and chill, preferably overnight.

NOTE: This recipe is also excellent when made with pork and beef. The cut for the beef should be eye of round or bottom round.

BACCALÀ TRICOLORE
Tricolored Baccalà
Serves 8

Baccalà is salted cod. It must be soaked for several days to remove the salt; change the water every day. It is sold in Italian specialty stores, Korean food shops, and markets serving the Italian and Spanish populations.

2 pounds *baccalà*, soaked
1 onion, quartered
1 celery rib, halved
1 bunch fresh parsley
1 tablespoon capers
2 to 3 anchovy fillets
3 to 4 *cornichons* or 1 sour pickle
1 large garlic clove
1 shallot or 1 small onion
1 tablespoon red wine vinegar
½ cup olive oil
1 small potato, boiled, peeled, and quartered
1 red bell pepper, roasted and skinned, or 1 small jar of pimientos, for decoration

1. Remove and discard the skin and bones from the salt cod. Cut into 2-inch chunks.
2. In a casserole, combine the cod, onion, celery, and 2 to 3 parsley sprigs. Add water to cover and bring to a boil over high heat. Reduce the heat to low and simmer for about 10 minutes. Cool and remove the cod to a serving dish with a slotted spoon.
3. In a food processor or blender, combine 2 parsley sprigs, the capers, anchovies, *cornichons* or pickle, garlic, shallot, and vinegar. Process until chopped very fine. Add the oil slowly, dropping in the pieces of potato one at a time while adding the oil. Pour the sauce over the fish and decorate with the red pepper, cut into strips, and the remaining parsley sprigs.

1 pound *baccalà*, soaked
1 cup olive oil
1 garlic clove, sliced
Freshly ground pepper
¹/₄ cup heavy cream
2 to 3 parsley sprigs, minced

BACCALÀ MANTECATO
Creamed Salt Cod
Serves 6

1. Drain the *baccalà* and plunge it into a pot of boiling water. Reduce the heat to low and simmer for 20 minutes. Drain, cool, and discard the skin and bones.
2. Flake the fish into small pieces and place in a food processor or blender. Turn the machine on and start adding the oil drop by drop, as you would for a mayonnaise. With the machine running, add the garlic, pepper, and the remaining oil. Stop as soon as mixture is creamy; do not overprocess.
3. Place a little oil in the top of a double boiler set over hot water. Add the processed *baccalà* and cook, stirring, until heated through.
4. Add the cream and continue cooking for a few minutes until hot. Add the minced parsley and serve hot.

NOTE: If you wish to serve *baccalà* at room temperature, omit the cream. To use less oil, start processing the fish with ¹/₄ cup milk.

¹/₄ cup olive oil, plus 2 tablespoons for oiling pan
1 large onion, coarsely chopped
1 garlic clove, peeled
¹/₄ cup dry white wine
3 anchovies, chopped, or 1 teaspoon anchovy paste
2 to 3 parsley sprigs, minced
6 tablespoons butter
2 cups milk
2¹/₂ pounds *baccalà* soaked
³/₄ cup all-purpose flour
Freshly ground pepper
Pinch of cinnamon
2 tablespoons freshly grated Parmesan cheese
Fresh parsley, for garnish

BACCALÀ ALLA VICENTINA
Salt Cod Vicenza Style
Serves 6

1. In a large saucepan, combine oil with the onion and garlic. Sauté over moderate heat until the onion is soft and translucent, about 5 minutes. Add the wine, cover, and cook over moderately low heat until the wine evaporates and the onion is creamed. Discard the garlic. Add the anchovies and parsley and cook briefly. Off the heat, stir in the butter until it dissolves. Stir in the milk and let cool.

2. Preheat the oven to 350°. Generously oil a baking pan that will hold the *baccalà* snugly. Cut the fish into serving pieces and pat dry.

3. In a mixing bowl, combine the flour, a good grinding of pepper, the cinnamon, and the Parmesan. Dredge the *baccalà* pieces in the flour mixture and set in a single layer in the prepared pan. Pour the onion-milk sauce over the fish. Bake until the *baccalà* starts to flake and the sauce is reduced, 35 to 40 minutes. Do not let the fish dry out. Add more milk, if necessary.

4. Serve hot, garnished with parsley.

NOTE: In Vicenza, this dish is always served with polenta, preferably the white corn type.

CAPESANTE AL PESTO
Scallops with Pesto
Serves 6

1 pound bay scallops or sea scallops
2 tablespoons unsalted butter
Pinch of freshly ground white pepper
Juice of ½ lemon
1 tablespoon chopped capers
3 to 4 tablespoons Pesto Sauce base (see page 114),
    without cheese
Crusty Italian bread, sliced

1. Wash and drain the scallops. If using large ones, cut them in half. Pat dry.

2. In a large skillet, melt the butter over moderate heat. Add the scallops and cook just until they become opaque, 2 to 3 minutes. Sprinkle with the pepper and lemon juice. Add the capers and *pesto* and cook until just heated through.

3. Serve at once, with slices of bread.

NOTE: This recipe can be served cold. Just substitute olive oil for the butter when cooking the scallops.

This is a Roman specialty and is usually served with *"pan dorato"* (golden bread)—bread croutons dipped in a light batter and fried.

2 tablespoons all-purpose flour
1/4 teaspoon powdered sage
Freshly ground pepper
1 1/2 pounds fresh medium shrimp, shelled and deveined
1/2 cup olive oil
Juice of 1 lemon
3/4 cup Marsala or sherry wine
1 tablespoon tomato paste
1 tablespoon minced fresh parsley

1. In a shallow plate, combine the flour, sage, and pepper. Dredge the shrimp in the seasoned flour, shaking off any excess.
2. In a skillet large enough to contain shrimp in one layer, heat the oil over moderate heat. Add the shrimp and sauté, tossing, until they turn pink. Stir in half of the lemon juice and remove the shrimp with a slotted spoon. Keep warm.
3. Add the wine to the skillet and deglaze over moderate heat, scraping up the brown bits that cling to the skillet. Stir in the tomato paste and simmer for 8 to 10 minutes. Return the shrimp to the skillet and add remaining lemon juice and parsley. Stir until warmed through and serve at once.

COZZE ALLA TARANTINA
Taranto-Style Mussels
Serves 6

3 pounds mussels, scrubbed and debearded
1 tablespoon all-purpose flour
1/4 cup plus 2 tablespoons olive oil
2 garlic cloves, sliced
4 to 5 fresh tomatoes—peeled, seeded, and coarsely chopped—or use peeled, canned tomatoes
A few flakes of *diavoletto* (Italian hot red pepper flakes, optional)
3/4 cup dry white wine
Freshly ground pepper
2 to 3 fresh parsley sprigs, minced

1. Place the mussels in a large bowl. Add water to cover and sprinkle on the flour. Set the bowl in the refrigerator for at least 1 hour. Rinse the mussels thoroughly before using them.

2. In a large skillet, warm the oil over moderate heat. Add the garlic, tomatoes, and *diavoletto* and cook for 10 minutes. Add the mussels and stir in the wine. Cover and cook until the mussels open, 10 to 15 minutes. Discard any mussels that do not open. Season to taste with pepper and sprinkle with the parsley. Serve hot.

COZZE CON LA SALSA VERDE
Mussels in Green Sauce
Serves 6

42 large fresh mussels, well scrubbed and debearded
2 *cornichons* or 1 small pickle
1 tablespoon capers
1 garlic clove
1 anchovy fillet
1 hard-cooked egg, quartered
1 teaspoon grainy mustard
2 tablespoons fresh lemon juice
1 teaspoon Worcestershire sauce
Freshly ground pepper
$2/3$ cup olive oil

1. In a skillet, set the mussels over moderate heat until they open. Shake the pan occasionally. Remove the open mussels to a bowl and discard half of the shells. Reserve the liquid and strain it through a double thickness of dampened cheesecloth. Discard any mussels that do not open.

2. In a food processor or blender, combine the *cornichons*, capers, garlic, anchovy, egg, mustard, lemon juice, Worcestershire, and pepper to taste. Purée, adding the oil gradually during processing. Add a little of the reserved mussel liquor, just enough to loosen the sauce.

3. Set the mussels in the half shell on a serving platter and spoon some of the sauce over each mussel. Serve as is or chilled.

NOTE: This sauce also can be used as a dip for shrimp or vegetables.

Giulianova is a charming holiday resort on the
Adriatic Coast in Abruzzo.

ANTIPASTO ALLA GIULIESE
Antipasto à la Giulianova
Serves 6

1 pound squid, cleaned
3/4 pound scrod, cod, sole, or flounder
1 pound medium shrimp, shelled and deveined
1/2 pound mussels or clams, or both, well scrubbed and
 debearded
3/4 cup olive oil
Juice of 1 lemon
1 can (7 ounces) tunafish, drained
1 teaspoon anchovy paste
1 tablespoon capers
1 or 2 pickled peppers or 1 pickle
1 or 2 garlic cloves
1 tablespoon red wine vinegar
Salt and freshly ground pepper
4 or 5 sprigs fresh parsley, chopped

1. In a large pot of boiling water, cook the squid, fish, and
shrimp for about 5 minutes. Allow to cool in the cooking water.
Cut the squid into rings, divide the tentacles, flake the fish, cut
the shrimp into two or three pieces, and set aside.
2. In a skillet, place the mussels or clams over moderate heat. As
soon as the shells start to open, remove the mollusks from the
heat and discard the shells. Discard any that do not open.
3. In a serving bowl, arrange the squid, fish, and mussels or
clams.
4. In a food processor or blender, combine the oil, lemon juice,
tuna, anchovy paste, capers, peppers or pickle, garlic, and vinegar. Process until smooth and season to taste with the salt and
pepper. Pour the sauce on the fish. Add the parsley, toss well, and
chill.
5. Serve the antipasto chilled, sprinkled with additional parsley. If you wish, decorate with lettuce leaves and tomato slices.

ANTIPASTO DI POLPI
Octopus Antipasto
Serves 6

1 bay leaf
10 peppercorns
1 teaspoon distilled white vinegar
2 pounds cleaned octopus
Juice of 1 lemon
¼ cup olive oil
Salt and freshly ground pepper
1 tablespoon red wine vinegar (optional)
2 to 3 sprigs fresh parsley, chopped, for garnish

1. In an enameled or other nonreactive casserole large enough to contain the octopus, combine the bay leaf, peppercorns, vinegar, and 4 cups of water over moderately high heat. Bring to a boil.

2. Spear the octopus above the neck with a fork and dip in and out of the boiling water several times. As soon as the tentacles curl up, slide the *polpi* into the water. Remove from the heat, cover, and let stand, unrefrigerated, for about 8 hours. Refrigerate, until chilled or overnight.

3. Rinse the *polpi* well, running your fingers along the tentacles and squeezing out any accumulated mucus or sand. Wrap in a damp cloth and refrigerate.

4. In a mixing bowl, combine the lemon juice, olive oil, salt and pepper to taste, and the vinegar. Mix well.

5. Cut the octopus diagonally into ¼-inch pieces. Add to the dressing and toss well. Turn the antipasto onto a serving dish, sprinkle with the parsley, and decorate as you wish, with lettuce or tomato or both.

NOTE: Shrimp, scallops, or other seafood may be added to this antipasto. Poach them briefly in the boiling water and combine after chilling.

¾ pound filleted flaky fish such as flounder, perch, haddock, or scrod, poached (see NOTE)

4 to 5 squid, cleaned, skinned, and poached (see NOTE)

12 mussels, steamed (see NOTE)

8 to 10 shrimp, poached (see NOTE)

1 teaspoon Dijon-style mustard

2 tablespoons mayonnaise, preferably homemade (see page 41)

Lemon juice

2 tablespoons drained and chopped capers

2 to 3 parsley sprigs, minced

1 *cornichon* or sour pickle, chopped

1 garlic clove, mashed (optional)

¼ cup plus 1 tablespoon olive oil

Freshly ground pepper

1 head romaine lettuce, for garnish

2 lemons, cut into wedges, for garnish

1. In a large bowl, flake the fish fillets. Cut the squid into thin rounds and the tentacles into strips. Add the squid to the bowl.

2. Remove the mussels from their shells and add the mussels to the bowl; discard the shells. Dice the shrimp and add along with the mustard, mayonnaise, lemon juice to taste, the capers, parsley, *cornichon* or pickle, garlic, oil, and pepper to taste. Mix thoroughly and chill.

3. Serve on lettuce leaves, garnished with lemon wedges.

NOTE: Here are my methods for poaching and steaming fish and shellfish.

• *Poaching:* In a large casserole, combine 1 small onion, quartered; 1 celery rib; 1 parsley sprig; 1 sliced carrot; 1 garlic clove; 4 to 5 peppercorns; salt; and a shot of vinegar. Add 4 cups water and bring the mixture to a boil. Add the tougher, larger fish, such as squid, first and remove as soon as the fish is tender and/or flaky.

• *Steaming:* Place the scrubbed shellfish (mussels, clams, etc.) in a large skillet and cook over moderate heat. Remove the skillet as soon as the shells open; discard any mussels that don't open. Strain the liquor through a double thickness of dampened cheesecloth and add to the fish broth.

TOTANI RIPIENI
Stuffed Squid
Serves 6

6 squid, cleaned and washed
$^{1}/_{2}$ cup olive oil
3 garlic cloves, peeled
$^{1}/_{2}$ cup Gaeta or Greek olives, pitted
1 tablespoon capers
1 to 2 parsley sprigs
1 cup fine dry bread crumbs
1 teaspoon anchovy paste
Salt and freshly ground pepper
$^{3}/_{4}$ cup dry white wine
1 tablespoon minced fresh parsley

1. Finely chop the squid tentacles. In a large skillet, heat $^{1}/_{4}$ cup of the oil over moderate heat. Add the tentacles and cook, stirring, for about 15 minutes.
2. On a cutting board, combine the garlic, olives, capers, and parsley. Chop coarsely and add to the skillet. Cook for 3 minutes. Add the bread crumbs and cook until the mixture is well blended. Add the anchovy paste and season to taste with salt and pepper. Remove from the heat and set aside to cool.
3. Fill each squid half full with the cooled mixture. Secure with toothpicks. (Do not overstuff the squid; they might burst during cooking.)
4. In a casserole, warm the remaining $^{1}/_{4}$ cup oil over moderate heat. Add the squid in a single layer and cook for 10 minutes, turning once. Sprinkle any remaining stuffing over the squid or use about 1 tablespoon bread crumbs.
5. Pour in the wine, cover, and cook over medium heat until the squid are done, about 1 hour. If the liquid evaporates, add a little water. When cooked, a bit of sauce should remain.
6. Serve hot, sprinkled with the parsley

NOTE: This dish is also good at room temperature. The squid can be sliced and served cold.

6 boneless, skinless chicken breasts
1 leek, washed, trimmed, and cut into rounds
1 bay leaf
Salt and freshly ground pepper
Juice of ¹/₂ lemon

SAUCE
1 cup loosely packed Italian parsley leaves
¹/₂ cup loosely packed fresh basil leaves
1 garlic clove
1 tablespoon capers
2 to 3 *cornichons* or 1 small sour pickle
1 celery rib, coarsely chopped
¹/₂ cup virgin olive oil
1 tablespoon red wine vinegar
Juice of ¹/₂ lemon

POLLO AL VERDE
Green Chicken
Serves 6

1. In a large steamer with the rack set over about 1 inch of water, place the chicken breasts in one layer. Scatter on the leek, bay leaf, salt and pepper, and lemon juice to taste. Cook for 30 minutes and cool. Reserve the cooking liquid.

2. In a food processor or blender, combine all of the sauce ingredients except the lemon juice. Purée until very fine. (If the sauce seems too dense, add a few tablespoons of the cooking liquid.) Taste the sauce and add lemon juice as needed.

3. On a serving dish, arrange the chicken breasts. Discard the leek and bay leaf. Pour the sauce over the chicken and serve at room temperature.

NOTE: This dish can be decorated with tomato slices, radishes, or roasted red and yellow bell peppers, if you desire.

ANTIPASTO DI FEGATINI ALL' ABRUZZESE
Chicken Livers Abruzzo
Serves 4 to 6

3 tablespoons olive oil
1 large onion, thinly sliced
¼ cup dry white wine
1 or 2 *cornichons,* chopped, or 1 small sour pickle
1 pound chicken livers, trimmed and cut bite-sized
Pinch of sugar
Salt and freshly ground pepper

1. In a large skillet, warm the oil over moderate heat. Add the onion and toss with the oil. Cover and cook over low heat until the onion is soft and translucent, 5 to 7 minutes. While the onion cooks, add the wine a little at a time. Stir in the *cornichons* or pickle, and cook briefly. Add the chicken livers and season with the sugar and salt and pepper to taste. Simmer until the livers are done, about 8 minutes. Do not overcook.
2. Serve hot in individual dishes.

NOTE: I like to serve this antipasto with drinks at my coffee table. Everyone seems to need a snack with drinks, and I prefer this to more ordinary cheese or nuts.

SALSICCE ALLO SPIEDO
Skewered Sausages
Serves 6

6 Italian sausages
6 bay leaves

1. Using long skewers, alternate each sausage with 1 bay leaf.
2. Cook over a barbecue grill or under a hot broiler, turning often, until the sausages are done, about 45 minutes.
3. Discard bay leaves. Serve hot, off the skewers.

2 *cotechini* or other spicy pork sausage (about 1 pound each)
1 onion, cross-cut at the root end
1 celery rib
1 parsley sprig
1 carrot
1 bay leaf
10 to 12 peppercorns
Pinch of thyme
Minced fresh parsley, for garnish

COTECHINO DELLA VIGILIA DI CAPODANNO
New Year's Eve Cotechino
Serves 12

1. Pierce the *cotechini* in several places to prevent them from exploding. In a large stockpot, combine the sausages with the onion, celery, parsley sprig, carrot, bay leaf, peppercorns, and thyme. Add water to cover and bring to a boil over high heat. Reduce the heat to low and simmer for about 1 hour. Allow to cool in the cooking liquid.
2. Serve warm or at room temperature, garnished with the minced parsley.

NOTE: *Cotechino* is usually served with lentils and they are traditionally eaten on the first and last day of the year because lentils represent money and success in business. The dish is decorated with parsley, which Romans (ancient and modern) believe wards off evil spirits.

It might not be everybody's cup of stew, but for the cognoscenti this is one of the most famous Tuscan specialties, and I love it.

TRIPPA ALLA FIORENTINA
Tripe Florentine Style
Serves 6 to 8

6 tablespoons olive oil
2 tablespoons chopped prosciutto
4½ pounds tripe, washed and cut into strips
½ cup dry red wine
1 onion, coarsely chopped
1 celery rib, coarsely chopped

1 carrot, coarsely chopped
Salt and freshly ground pepper
1 can (24 ounces) tomato purée (see NOTE)
Freshly grated Parmesan cheese

1. In a casserole, warm the oil over moderately high heat. Add the prosciutto and sauté briefly. Add the tripe and cook until the tripe starts to stick to the bottom of the casserole. Add the wine and boil until it evaporates.

2. Add the onion, celery, and carrot and season to taste with salt and pepper. Cook, stirring, over moderate heat, for 10 minutes.

3. Add the tomato purée and rinse the can with about 1/4 cup water. Add the water to the tripe. Stir, cover, and cook over low heat until the tripe is tender, about 2 hours. (The cooking time will depend on the quality of tripe; it may take as long as 4 hours for this amount.)

4. Serve the stew sprinkled with Parmesan cheese.

NOTE: You can use canned peeled tomatoes if you wish. In that case, add 2 teaspoons tomato paste just after the wine evaporates. Also, this tripe dish is much tastier the next day. To reheat, bring the stew to a simmer and cook gently for 10 minutes.

Pastas

4 tablespoons unsalted butter
1 tablespoon olive oil
1 large onion, chopped
¼ cup dry white wine
¼ pound *pancetta* or bacon, diced
3 eggs
4 to 5 parsley sprigs, minced
1 pound spaghetti
½ cup freshly grated Parmesan cheese
Freshly ground pepper

SPAGHETTI ALLA CARBONARA
Spaghetti Tossed with Bacon, Butter, Eggs, and Cheese
Serves 6

1. In a skillet, melt the butter with the oil over low heat. Add the onion and sauté until soft and translucent. Do not allow the onion to color. Stir in the wine and the *pancetta,* and cook until the wine evaporates.

2. In a large serving bowl, beat the eggs with the parsley; set aside.

3. In a large pot of salted boiling water, cook the spaghetti according to package directions until just *al dente*. Drain and turn into the serving bowl. Toss the spaghetti with the egg mixture. Add the Parmesan and the onion-*pancetta* mixture. Sprinkle with a liberal amount of pepper and serve immediately.

SPAGHETTI ALLA CONTADINA
Spaghetti Peasant Style
Serves 6

¹/₄ pound dried tomatoes, coarsely chopped
2 onions, chopped
1 garlic clove, minced
4 tablespoons olive oil
1 teaspoon tomato paste
¹/₄ cup dry red wine or water
A few flakes of *diavoletto* (Italian hot red pepper flakes, optional)
Salt and freshly ground pepper
1 pound spaghetti or linguine
2 to 3 fresh parsley sprigs, minced

1. In a large skillet, combine the tomatoes, onions, garlic, and 2 tablespoons of the oil. Cover and cook, stirring occasionally, over low heat for 20 minutes.
2. Dilute the tomato paste with the wine and add it to the skillet. Add *diavoletto* and season to taste with salt and pepper. Cover and cook until the tomatoes and onions are tender, 25 to 30 minutes. Add the remaining 2 tablespoons oil and remove from the heat.
3. Meanwhile, in a large pot of salted boiling water, cook the pasta according to package directions, until just *al dente*. Drain well and turn into a serving bowl. Pour the sauce over the pasta and sprinkle with the parsley.

1 large red onion
1 small celery rib
1 garlic clove
1 to 2 parsley sprigs
¼ cup plus 2 tablespoons olive oil
Salt and freshly ground pepper
1 pound chicken gizzards, cut in half
1 cup dry wine, preferably red
2 tablespoons tomato paste
About 2 cups hot chicken broth
1 pound spaghetti

SPAGHETTI DEL POLLAIOLO
Poultry Man's Spaghetti
Serves 6

1. In a food processor or blender, finely chop the onion, celery, garlic, and parsley.
2. In a terra-cotta or enameled casserole, warm the olive oil over moderate heat. Add the chopped vegetables and sauté for about 30 minutes. Add the chicken gizzards and cook for 30 minutes. Season to taste with salt and pepper.
3. Add the wine and cook until evaporated. Add the tomato paste and stir well. Pour in 1 cup of the broth, cover, and simmer until the gizzards are done, about 45 minutes. Add additional broth, if necessary.
4. Remove the gizzards and chop them in a food processor or blender. Return to the casserole, add the remaining 1 cup broth, and simmer until the sauce is quite thick and smooth.
5. In a large pot of salted boiling water, cook the spaghetti according to package directions, until just *al dente*. Drain and dress with sauce, before serving.

SPAGHETTI PRIMAVERA
Springtime Spaghetti
Serves 6

I am a little fed up with pasta Primavera. When done with care it is good, but often it is only a mishmash of dubious origin. Not this Primavera—which is a superb reflection of Sirio Maccione's exquisite taste and a favorite of the chic clientele of his well-known New York City restaurant, Le Cirque. It is with Sirio's kind permission that I use this recipe.

1 bunch broccoli
2 small zucchini
4 asparagus spears
1^1/$_2$ cups green beans, trimmed and cut into 1-inch pieces
^{1}/$_2$ cup fresh or frozen peas
^{1}/$_2$ cup snow peas
1 tablespoon vegetable oil
2 cups thinly sliced mushrooms
Salt and freshly ground pepper
1 teaspoon chopped hot red or green chili peppers or ^{1}/$_2$ teaspoon *diavoletto* (Italian hot red pepper flakes, optional)
^{1}/$_4$ cup finely chopped parsley
6 tablespoons olive oil
1 teaspoon finely chopped garlic
3 cups ripe tomatoes, cut into 1-inch cubes
6 fresh basil leaves, chopped, or 1 teaspoon dried basil
1 pound spaghetti or *spaghettini*
4 tablespoons butter
2 tablespoons chicken broth
^{1}/$_2$ cup heavy cream, or more
^{2}/$_3$ cup freshly grated Parmesan cheese
^{1}/$_3$ cup toasted pine nuts (*pignoli*)

1. Trim the broccoli and break it into bite-sized pieces.
2. Trim off and discard the ends of the zucchini. Do not peel. Cut the zucchini lengthwise into quarters, and cut each quarter into 1-inch pieces.
3. Cut each asparagus spear crosswise into thirds. Cook the broccoli, zucchini, asparagus, and green beans spears separately in boiling water until tender but crisp, about 5 minutes each.

Drain well and run under cold water to stop the cooking, and drain again. Combine the four vegetables in a mixing bowl.

4. Cook peas and snow peas in boiling water for 1 minute if fresh, or 30 seconds if frozen. Drain, cool under cold water, and drain again. Combine with the other vegetables.

5. In a large skillet, heat the vegetable oil over moderate heat. Add the mushrooms and salt and pepper to taste and cook for about 2 minutes. Add the diavoletto and the parsley and combine with the other vegetables in the mixing bowl; do not wash the skillet. Set aside.

6. In a saucepan, heat 3 tablespoons of the olive oil over moderate heat. Add half of the garlic, the tomatoes, and salt and pepper to taste. Cook for 4 minutes, stirring gently so as not to break up the tomatoes. Add the basil, stir, and set aside.

7. In the skillet, combine the remaining 3 tablespoons of olive oil with the remaining 1/2 teaspoon garlic and the vegetable mixture. Cook, stirring gently, until the vegetables are just heated through.

8. In a large pot of salted boiling water, cook the spaghetti until just *al dente*. Drain and return the spaghetti to the kettle.

9. Select a casserole or Dutch oven that is large enough to hold the spaghetti and all the vegetables. Melt the butter in it over low heat and add the chicken broth, 1/2 cup of the cream, and the cheese. Cook gently, stirring constantly, on and off the heat until smooth. Add the spaghetti and toss quickly to blend. Add half the vegetables and pour in the tomato mixture, tossing and stirring over very low heat. Add the remaining vegetables and, if the sauce seems too dry, add about 1/4 cup more cream. The sauce should not be soupy. Add the pine nuts and give the mixture one final toss.

10. Serve in warm soup or spaghetti bowls.

PASTA AL PESTO
Pasta with Pesto
Serves 6

1 pound spaghetti, linguine, *trenette*, or *perciatelli*
2 tablespoons unsalted butter

PESTO SAUCE

3 cups loosely packed fresh basil leaves
$1/2$ cup olive oil
Pinch of coarse (kosher) salt, if desired
3 garlic cloves
$1/2$ cup freshly grated Parmesan cheese
2 tablespoons pine nuts (*pignoli*)

1. In a large pot of salted boiling water, cook the pasta according to package directions, until just *al dente*.
2. Meanwhile, set the butter aside to soften.
3. In a food processor or blender, combine all of the *pesto* sauce ingredients and process to the consistency of cream. Turn the mixture into a serving bowl and add the softened butter.
4. Drain the pasta, reserving $1/2$ cup of the cooking water. Place the pasta in the serving bowl and toss with the *pesto*, adding some of the reserved cooking water to thin the mixture, if necessary. Serve with additional Parmesan if desired.

NOTE: This *pesto* sauce freezes well. When basil is in season, prepare the base for *pesto* by blending the leaves, oil, salt, and garlic in a food processor. Freeze in batches and mark the portions. Defrost and add the remaining ingredients, or use base as a flavoring for other sauces, vegetables, or stews.

For a more authentic pasta *al pesto*, drop 2 thinly sliced potatoes into the boiling pot of water. Cook for 5 minutes and add the pasta. Drain together and toss the pasta and potato slices with the sauce.

Lia Saraceni is a sophisticated lady, a wife, the mother of two charming youngsters, and a dedicated doctor. She is also a gracious hostess who loves to cook. She is not at all amused at being "immortalized," as she put it, by the name of a recipe dedicated to certain ladies of the night; nevertheless, she gave me her recipe. Until I get the recipe for her famous stuffed rabbit, this will have to do.

SPAGHETTI ALLA PUTTANESCA LIA SARACENI
Lia Saraceni's Spaghetti with Harlots' Sauce
Serves 6

1/4 cup olive oil
1 garlic clove
A few flakes of *diavoletto* (Italian hot red pepper flakes, optional)
1 can (7 ounces) Italian tunafish
1 can (16 ounces) peeled tomatoes, drained and chopped
1 small jar (6 ounces) mushrooms in oil, chopped
1 can (8 ounces) pitted black or green olives, sliced
1 tablespoon capers
Pinch of oregano
1 pound spaghetti

1. In a large skillet, combine the oil, garlic, and *diavoletto* over moderate heat. Sauté until the garlic is slightly colored. Remove the garlic and *diavoletto* and discard.

2. Add the tuna and its oil and cook for 5 minutes, flaking the fish with a fork. Add the tomatoes and cook until the liquid is absorbed. Add the mushrooms, olives, and capers and cook 5 minutes, just to heat through. Add the oregano and remove from the heat.

3. Meanwhile, in a large pot of salted boiling water, cook the spaghetti according to package directions, until just *al dente*. Drain, dress with the sauce, toss, and serve.

PASTA ALLA NERANO
Nerano-Style Pasta
Serves 6

Nerano is a town on the Amalfi Drive—or even better, it is one of Amalfi's gems.

8 tablespoons (1 stick) unsalted butter
1 tablespoon oil
2 pounds zucchini, sliced about $1/4$ inch thick
1 egg yolk
$1/4$ cup heavy cream
1 tablespoon minced fresh basil or $1/4$ teaspoon dried
1 pound spaghetti
4 ounces mozzarella cheese, diced
Freshly grated Parmesan cheese

1. In a large skillet, melt 4 tablespoons of the butter with the oil over moderate heat. Add the zucchini and sauté until soft, 4 to 5 minutes. Turn into a large serving bowl. (This step can be done in advance.)

2. In a bowl, beat the egg yolk and cream together. Pour over the zucchini, add the basil, and toss.

3. In a large pot of salted boiling water, cook the spaghetti according to package directions, until *al dente*. Drain the pasta, reserving 1 cup of the cooking water.

4. Add the pasta to the zucchini and mix. Add the remaining 4 tablespoons butter and the mozzarella. Toss again and serve with the Parmesan on the side.

Adi Giovannetti of New York's Il Nido serves a pasta *all'Amatriciana*, which is absolutely delicious. When I first ate it, I caused Adi to pale. When he asked whether or not I liked the dish, I answered: "I hate it; it is made with the wrong pasta, the wrong ingredients, and it is better than mine." Here is my version—a little more authentic if you use *pancetta* and, I hope, equally delicious.

PASTA ALL' AMATRICIANA
Amatrice-Style Pasta
Serves 6

2 tablespoons olive oil
1 onion, finely chopped
1/4 pound *pancetta* (Italian bacon) or prosciutto, in one slice, diced
1/4 cup dry white wine, preferably Frascati
1 teaspoon tomato paste
1 pound fresh plum tomatoes, peeled, seeded, and chopped, or 1 can (16 ounces) peeled Italian plum tomatoes
Freshly ground pepper
A few flakes of *diavoletto* (Italian hot red pepper flakes, optional)
1 pound spaghetti
Freshly grated Pecorino Romano cheese, or a combination of Pecorino and Parmesan

1. In a heatproof casserole, warm the oil over low heat. Add the onion and cook until the onion is soft and translucent, about 5 minutes. Add the *pancetta* or prosciutto and cook briefly. Add the wine and cook until it evaporates.

2. Stir in the tomato paste, tomatoes, pepper to taste, and the *diavoletto*. Bring to a boil over moderate heat, reduce the heat to low, and simmer for 15 minutes.

3. Meanwhile, in a pot of salted boiling water, cook the pasta according to package directions, until just *al dente*. Drain and dress the pasta with the sauce. Pass the cheese separately.

PASTA CON LE SARDE ALLA PALERMITANA
Palermo-Style Pasta with Sardines
Serves 6

A unique Sicilian recipe which even in Italy is relatively unknown. It is not easy to find fresh sardines in this country, but if you do, try this recipe.

3 small or 2 medium fennel bulbs, tough stems removed, tender part cut in wedges
Coarse (kosher) salt
1½ tablespoons white raisins
1 large onion, finely chopped
¼ cup olive oil
1 tablespoon tomato paste
1½ tablespoons pine nuts
¾ pound fresh sardines, cleaned and filleted
Salt and freshly ground pepper
2 anchovy fillets (optional)
1 pound spaghetti, *bavette*, or *perciatelli*

1. In a large pot, bring water to a boil. Plunge the fennel into it and boil for 10 minutes. Add some salt, stir, and remove the fennel to a colander. Remove ½ cup of the water and soak the raisins in it. Set the remaining water aside.
2. In a saucepan, combine the onion with water to cover and add a pinch of salt. Cook, covered, over moderate heat until tender. Stir occasionally. Add the oil, tomato paste, pine nuts, and the soaked raisins and cook for 10 minutes. Add the sardines and cook for 10 minutes. Add the fennel and cook over low heat, turning the sardines from time to time.
3. Bring the reserved water to a boil and cook the pasta according to the package directions, until just *al dente*. Drain and dress with the sauce; let rest a few minutes before serving.

1 pound mussels, well scrubbed and debearded
¼ cup plus 1 tablespoon olive oil
1 parsley sprig
1 large garlic clove
1 teaspoon tomato paste
1 can (8 ounces) tomato sauce
1 pound spaghetti or linguine
¼ cup minced fresh parsley

1. In a large skillet, place the mussels over moderate heat. When the mussels begin to open, remove the opened ones immediately. Discard the shells and reserve the mussels in one bowl and their liquor in another. Set both bowls aside. Discard mussels that do not open.

2. In a saucepan, combine the oil, parsley sprig, and garlic over moderate heat. As soon as the garlic begins to fry, add the reserved mussels and cook briefly, 2 to 3 minutes.

3. Strain the mussel liquor through a double thickness of dampened cheesecloth. Stir the tomato paste into this liquid and add to the saucepan with the mussels. Stir well and add the tomato sauce. Cover the skillet, reduce the heat to low, and simmer for 15 minutes.

4. In a large pot of salted boiling water, cook the pasta according to package directions, until just *al dente*. Drain well, turn into a serving bowl, and dress with the mussel sauce. Sprinkle with the minced parsley and serve. Do *not* serve with cheese.

Here is my own version of this popular pasta.

1 large package (8 ounces) cream cheese, at room temperature
Good pinch of basil
Good pinch of oregano
½ cup minced fresh parsley
¼ cup **Bolognese Sauce** (see page 38) or other tomato sauce (optional)

PAGLIA E FIENO ALLA ANNA TERESA
Straw and Hay à la Anna Teresa
Serves 6

1 garlic clove, minced
³/₄ cup heavy cream
¹/₂ pound homemade green noodles
¹/₂ pound homemade egg noodles
Freshly ground Parmesan cheese

1. In a pasta serving bowl, combine the cream cheese, basil, oregano, parsley, sauce, garlic, and heavy cream. Beat until smooth.

2. In a large pot of salted boiling water, cook the pasta until just *al dente*. Drain, reserving 1 cup of the cooking water.

3. Turn the pasta into the bowl and toss in the sauce. If the pasta seems too dry, add some of the cooking water. Serve with the Parmesan cheese.

LINGUINE O SPAGHETTI AL SUGO DI SEPPIE
Linguine or Spaghetti with Squid Sauce
Serves 6

¹/₄ cup olive oil
2 garlic cloves, peeled
³/₄ pound squid, cleaned and cut into rounds, tentacles divided
1 cup white wine
2 anchovy fillets, chopped
1 can (16 ounces) peeled Italian plum tomatoes
1 pound linguine or spaghetti
4 fresh parsley sprigs, minced

1. In a saucepan, warm the oil over moderate heat. Add the garlic and stir. As soon as the garlic begins to fry, add the squid. Cook briefly, stirring all the while. Add the wine and cook until it evaporates. Stir in the anchovies and tomatoes, breaking the tomatoes up with a wooden spoon. Reduce the heat to low and simmer, covered, for 30 minutes, or until squid are tender. If the sauce seems watery, remove the lid from the saucepan.

2. Meanwhile, in a large pot of salted boiling water, cook the pasta according to package directions, until just *al dente*. Drain well and dress with the sauce. Sprinkle with fresh chopped parsley and serve. No cheese, please!

1 pound mussels or clams (or a mixture of both), scrubbed and debearded
1/2 cup olive oil
2 large garlic cloves
2 tablespoons minced fresh Italian flat-leaf parsley
A few flakes of *diavoletto* (Italian hot red pepper flakes, optional)
1 pound squid, cleaned, skinned, cut into rings, and tentacles divided
1/2 cup dry white wine
1/2 pound small shrimp, shelled and coarsely chopped
Salt and freshly ground pepper
1 pound linguine or spaghetti

LINGUINE DEL PESCATORE
Fisherman's Linguine
Serves 6

1. Put a large pot of water on to boil.

2. In a large skillet, place the mussels over moderately high heat. As soon as they begin to open, transfer to a bowl. Remove the mussels from the shells and reserve the liquor in a bowl. Discard the shells and any mussels that do not open. If the mussels are large, halve them. Strain the liquor through a double thickness of dampened cheesecloth to remove any trace of sand.

3. Rinse the skillet and dry it. Add the oil and garlic and place over moderately high heat. As soon as the garlic begins to color, add 1 tablespoon of the parsley, the *diavoletto*, and the squid. Sauté, stirring, just briefly, 2 to 3 minutes. Add the wine and reserved mussel liquor and cook over moderate heat until hot. Add the shrimp and cook until the bits turn pink, 2 to 3 minutes. Add the mussels and cook for 2 minutes. Stir in the remaining 1 tablespoon parsley and season to taste with salt and pepper. Remove from heat, but keep the mixture warm.

4. Drop the pasta into the boiling water and cook according to package directions until just *al dente*.

5. Drain the pasta and dress it with the sauce. Serve at once.

NOTE: In Italy, this dish is *never* served with cheese.

TAGLIOLINI AL QUATTRO FORMAGGI
Noodles with Four Cheeses
Serves 6

Alfredo Viazzi, owner of Trattoria da Alfredo in New York's Greenwich Village, inspired this recipe. He is the inventor—I only adjusted the recipe to my own taste.

8 tablespoons (1 stick) unsalted butter
$1/4$ teaspoon white pepper
Pinch of freshly grated nutmeg
$1/4$ pound Fontina cheese, cubed
$1/4$ pound Gorgonzola cheese, crumbled
$1/4$ pound Robbiola cheese, cubed
1 cup freshly grated Parmesan cheese
1 cup heavy cream
$1^1/2$ pounds homemade *tagliolini* or packaged egg
  tagliolini
Freshly ground pepper

1. In a heavy deep saucepan, melt the butter over moderate heat. Season with the pepper and nutmeg. Add the Fontina, Gorgonzola, and Robbiola cheeses and stir until all have melted. Blend in $1/2$ cup of the Parmesan and the heavy cream. Stirring constantly with a wire whisk, cook for 5 minutes. Bring to a boil and set aside; keep warm.
2. In a large pot of salted boiling water, cook the *tagliolini* until just *al dente*. Drain and turn the pasta into a large warmed serving bowl. Toss well with the cheese sauce and serve at once, topped with the remaining $1/2$ cup of Parmesan and freshly ground pepper.

TAGLIATELLE AL LIMONE
Tagliatelle with Lemon
Serves 6 to 8

A true summer dish, delicate and surprising.

Minced zest of 1 large lemon
4 tablespoons unsalted butter
1 batch homemade pasta dough prepared with 6 eggs
2 cups heavy cream
Freshly grated Parmesan cheese

1. In a pasta serving bowl, combine the lemon zest and butter. Set aside in a warm place.

2. In a large pot of salted boiling water, cook the pasta until just *al dente*. Drain the pasta, reserving 1 cup of the cooking water. Turn the pasta into the serving bowl.

3. In a saucepan, heat the cream slightly and pour over the noodles. Toss gently but thoroughly and if the pasta seems dry, add some of the reserved water. Serve hot, with Parmesan cheese.

NOTE: Strips of prosciutto can be added to this dish, before tossing.

---

6 tablespoons unsalted butter
1 onion, finely chopped
3 tablespoons white wine or Cognac
1 batch spinach *tagliatelle*, made with 6 eggs
6 ounces smoked salmon, chopped or shredded
2 cups heavy cream
Freshly ground pepper

TAGLIATELLE VERDI AL SALMONE
Green Noodles with Salmon
Serves 6

1. In a large skillet, melt 3 tablespoons of the butter over moderate heat. Add the onion and cook, covered, over low heat until the onion is very soft. Do not let the onion brown. Add the wine and let evaporate.

2. In a large pot of salted boiling water, cook the pasta until just *al dente*.

3. Meanwhile, add the salmon to the skillet and stir over low heat for a few seconds. Add the cream and cook over very low heat until the sauce starts to boil.

4. Drain the pasta, reserving 1 cup of the cooking liquid.

5. In a serving bowl, dress the pasta with the cream sauce and grate pepper over it. If the mixture seems too dry, add a few tablespoons of the reserved cooking liquid. Add the remaining 3 tablespoons butter and toss to melt it. Serve immediately.

NOTE: The same *tagliatelle* can be dressed with Bolognese Sauce (page 38) to make the classic *tagliatelle alla Bolognese*.

TAGLIATELLE ALLA CAPRESE
Capri-Style Egg Noodles with Vegetables and Vodka
Serves 4

Gianni Minale, the *simpatico* owner of New York's Alfredo on the Park, is famous for his *risotto*, which he will make under your nose—if you ask him. Although I think that his *risotto* is superb, I simply adore this dish (which he indeed made under my nose). What a treat!

1 tablespoon olive oil
2 tablespoons unsalted butter
1 1/2 tablespoons finely chopped shallots
1 1/2 tablespoons finely chopped scallions
10 cherry tomatoes, stemmed and quartered
1/4 cup vodka
1 tablespoon dried basil
1 teaspoon dried green peppercorns, coarsely ground, or bottled green peppercorns in liquid, drained and crushed
1 cup chicken broth
3/4 pound *tagliatelle* or fettuccine
2 egg yolks
1/4 cup freshly grated Parmesan cheese, plus additional cheese for serving
2 tablespoons finely chopped parsley

1. In a large skillet, warm together the oil and butter over moderate heat. Add the shallots and scallions and cook briefly, stirring, until wilted. Add the tomatoes and cook, stirring, for about 3 minutes.
2. Add the vodka and ignite it. Add the basil, peppercorns, and broth and simmer for 5 minutes.
3. Meanwhile, in a large pot of salted boiling water, cook the pasta until just *al dente*. Drain.
4. Add the pasta to the sauce. Stir in the egg yolks and 1/4 cup cheese, tossing the pasta in the sauce. Let the sauce barely simmer over low heat until thickened; do not boil or the sauce might curdle. Stir in the parsley and serve with additional freshly grated Parmesan.

5 tablespoons unsalted butter
2 tablespoons olive oil
1 large onion, chopped
³/₄ pound chicken gizzards and hearts, chopped
2 Italian sausages (about ¹/₂ pound), crumbled
¹/₄ cup Marsala wine
¹/₄ pound chicken livers, diced (optional)
1 tablespoon tomato paste
³/₄ cup chicken broth
1 can (8 ounces) tomato sauce
¹/₂ cup heavy cream
1 batch *tagliatelle* made with 4 eggs
2 eggs, lightly beaten, or 4 egg whites
¹/₂ cup freshly grated Parmesan cheese
¹/₂ pound mozzarella cheese, chopped
¹/₂ pound smoked mozzarella cheese, chopped

PASTICCIO DI TAGLIATELLE ALLA FINANZIERA
Financier-Style Tagliatelle Timbale
Serves 6 to 8

1. In a large skillet, melt 2 tablespoons of the butter with the oil over moderate heat. Add the onion, gizzards and hearts, and sausages, and sauté until browned. Add the Marsala, cover, and cook over low heat until the wine is absorbed.

2. Add the livers and stir in the tomato paste, broth, and tomato sauce. Cover and simmer over low heat until the gizzards are tender, about 45 minutes. Add the cream, stir well, and remove from the heat.

3. In a large pot of salted boiling water, cook the pasta until just *al dente*. Drain, turn the pasta into a mixing bowl, and stir in the eggs. Toss gently but thoroughly. Add ¹/₄ cup of the Parmesan cheese while tossing. Add about one-third of the sauce and mix well.

4. Preheat the oven to 375°. Using 1 tablespoon of the remaining butter, butter two 9-inch pie dishes from which you can serve.

5. Place one-fourth of the pasta mixture on the bottom of each dish. Combine both mozzarella cheeses and scatter them over the *tagliatelle*. Top with one-third of the sauce, sprinkle with half of the remaining Parmesan, and cover with the remaining *tagliatelle* mixture. Finish with the remaining Parmesan and the remaining sauce. Dot with the remaining 2 tablespoons butter.

6. Bake for 20 to 25 minutes, until the top is nicely colored.

NOTE: This recipe is a good one for using up leftover noodles.

PASTA CON LA SALSA CRUDA
Pasta with Uncooked Sauce
Serves 6

Make the sauce at least two hours before you plan to serve it.

$^{1}/_{2}$ cup olive oil
1$^{1}/_{2}$ pounds fresh plum tomatoes, sliced
A few flakes of *diavoletto* (Italian hot red pepper flakes, optional)
$^{1}/_{2}$ cup sweet black olives, pitted and sliced
2 tablespoons minced fresh parsley
1 garlic clove, minced (optional)
Fresh basil or oregano, shredded
Freshly ground pepper
1 pound *rotelle* or *farfalle*

1. In a large serving bowl, combine the oil, tomatoes, *diavoletto*, olives, parsley, and garlic. Stir and season with basil or oregano, and pepper to taste. Set aside for at least 2 hours.
2. In a large pot of salted boiling water, cook the pasta according to package directions, until just *al dente*. Drain and turn the pasta into the bowl of sauce. Toss and serve.

NOTE: Pasta dressed this way can also be served at room temperature.

FARFALLE ROMANTICHE
Romantic Butterflies
Serves 6

Juice and grated zest of $^{1}/_{2}$ lemon
2 pounds fresh asparagus
6 tablespoons unsalted butter
1 cup heavy cream
12 thin slices prosciutto, cut into julienne
$^{3}/_{4}$ cup freshly grated Parmesan cheese
1$^{1}/_{2}$ pounds *farfalle*
Freshly ground pepper

1. In a large skillet, bring 2 inches of water to a boil. Add the lemon juice and zest. Add the asparagus and cook for 5 minutes. Drain and rinse under cold water.

2. Cut off about 1¹/₂ inches of the tips of the asparagus and set them aside. Purée the stalks in a food mill. Reserve the purée, discarding the tough fibers.

3. In a large skillet, melt the butter over moderate heat. Add the asparagus tips and sauté lightly for a few minutes. Add the cream and cook for 3 minutes. Add the asparagus purée and cook for 2 minutes. Add the prosciutto and blend gently. Add half of the Parmesan and stir in gently but thoroughly. Remove from the heat and keep warm.

4. In a large pot of salted boiling water, cook the *farfalle* according to package directions, until just *al dente*. Drain well, reserving 1 cup of the cooking water.

5. Add the pasta to the sauce in the skillet. Toss over low heat until the pasta is well coated, about 2 minutes. Serve with the remaining cheese and pass the pepper mill.

---

1 pound curly lasagne (with ruffled edges)
2 cups Béchamel Sauce (see page 42)
1 cup heavy cream
Pinch of freshly ground nutmeg
Freshly grated Parmesan cheese
¹/₂ pound smoked salmon, thinly sliced
3 tablespoons unsalted butter

PASTICCIO DI LASAGNE RICCE AL SALMONE
Curly Lasagne Timbale with Salmon
Serves 6 to 8

1. Butter a lasagna pan and set aside. Preheat the oven to 375°. In a large pot of salted boiling water, cook the lasagna strips, a few at a time, then plunge them into a bowl of cool water to stop the cooking, and drain on a damp tea towel.

2. In a bowl, combine the béchamel with the cream. Add the nutmeg and stir.

3. Arrange strips of the lasagne over the bottom of the prepared pan. Pour some of the béchamel on top and sprinkle with Parmesan. Add a few slices of salmon. Continue layering the pasta, cheese, and salmon until all of the pasta and salmon is used. Top with a good sprinkling of Parmesan and dot with the butter. Bake for about 35 to 40 minutes, until the top is nicely colored.

LASAGNE VERDI ALLA MODENESE
Modena-Style Green Lasagna
Serves 8

This is my favorite lasagna recipe; whoever has tried it has raved about it. It is a classic—and uncomplicated—Italian recipe from Modena.

2 cups Bolognese Sauce (see page 38)
1 batch green pasta dough made with 6 eggs
$^{1}/_{2}$ cup heavy cream
8 ounces mozzarella cheese, slivered
1 cup freshly grated Parmesan cheese
2 cups Béchamel Sauce (page 42)
2 tablespoons unsalted butter

1. Prepare the Bolognese Sauce in advance. All of the ingredients should be ready before cooking the lasagna.
2. Cut the pasta dough into wedges and roll each wedge through the pasta machine until as thin as possible. Using a paring knife or a toothed wheel, cut the sheets into strips $2^{1}/_{2}$ inches in width. Let the strips dry in the air on kitchen towels.
3. In a saucepan, warm the Bolognese Sauce and add the heavy cream to it. Remove from the heat and set aside.
4. Butter a baking dish or lasagna pan and cover the bottom with a ladleful of Bolognese Sauce. (Try to skim off only the liquid, leaving the meat, so that it won't stick when baked.) Set the pan aside.
5. In a large pot of boiling salted water, cook the lasagna a few strips at a time for a few minutes, then plunge them into a bowl of cool water to stop the cooking. Spread the strips on a clean, damp cloth to drain.
6. Cover the bottom of the baking dish with a layer of cooked lasagna. Scatter some of the mozzarella over, pour on some of the sauce, and sprinkle with a handful of Parmesan cheese. Continue layering until you fill the pan, spreading a thin layer of Béchamel Sauce when the pan is half filled. (At this point, the dish can be refrigerated.)
7. Preheat the oven to 375°. Just before it is baked, top with the remaining Béchamel Sauce, dot the surface with the butter, and sprinkle with the remaining Parmesan cheese. Bake for 45 minutes, until cooked through. Let set for 10 to 15 minutes before serving.

This dish is a specialty from the charming city of Lanciano, the town where I spent many summers and where in my youth I was named Miss Abruzzo. With my title, I had the right to participate in the Miss Italy competition, but Mother said No; she thought that Miss Abruzzo was enough. That same year Sophia Loren competed too, and she was elected Miss Cinema. What shall I say? Look, I really prefer to cook.

LASAGNE IN BRODO ALLA LANCIANESE
Lasagna in Broth Lanciano Style
Serves 8

About 2 cups hot homemade chicken broth (see page 130)
2 strips lemon zest
Pinch of cinnamon
1 batch homemade pasta dough, made with 4 eggs
1½ pounds mozzarella cheese, coarsely chopped
1¼ cups freshly grated Parmesan cheese
5 or 6 hard-cooked eggs, sliced
Tiny Meat Balls (page 143)

1. Place the chicken broth in a bowl and stir in the zest and cinnamon. Set aside.
2. Cut the pasta dough into wedges and roll each wedge through a pasta machine until as thin as possible. Using a paring knife or a fluted pastry wheel, cut the dough into 2½-inch strips.
3. Preheat the oven to 400°. Butter a lasagna pan generously. Line the pan with the uncooked strips of dough, letting the strips hang over. Sprinkle the dough with mozzarella, Parmesan, hard-cooked egg slices, meat balls, and ½ cup of the broth. Continue layering until you fill the pan. Sprinkle a large handful of the Parmesan over the top of the lasagna. Do not add any leftover broth.
4. Bake for about 30 minutes, or until the top is golden brown. Let set for about 10 minutes before cutting.

BRODO DI POLLO
Chicken Broth
Yields 2 to 3 quarts

1 chicken weighing 3 to 5 pounds
A few veal bones
1 onion with 2 cloves stuck in it
1 carrot
1 stalk of celery
1 or 2 sprigs of parsley
10 peppercorns
Salt

1. Place all ingredients in an 8–10 quart kettle or stock pot. Cover with cold water up to 4 inches above the solids. Bring to a boil and simmer for $2^{1}/_{2}$ hours. Strain broth into a bowl and chill. Reserve chicken and vegetables for another use.
2. Remove fat accumulated at the top of broth and use broth according to recipe.

NOTE: For a beef broth, substitute for the chicken 2 to 4 pounds of chuck, trimmed of fat, or use brisket.

MACCHERONI COL SUGHETTO ACERBO ALLA LELLA
Macaroni with Green and Red Sauce Lella
Serves 6

Lella's father, a lawyer and school superintendent, was my first respected and loved boss in Italy. His daughter Lella used to follow me around, as younger girls do with an older and, shall we say, popular one. Time has shortened the age difference, and now we are the best of friends on an equal basis. We even exchange recipes.

4 tablespoons olive oil
1 garlic clove, peeled
1 green bell pepper, cut into strips
1 red pepper, cut into strips
Pinch of rosemary
1 large onion, sliced
4 to 5 green tomatoes, peeled, seeded, and sliced
Pinch of basil

A few flakes of *diavoletto* (Italian hot red chili pepper
  flakes, optional)
Salt and freshly ground pepper
4 to 5 parsley sprigs, minced
1 pound *penne,* rigatoni, or ziti
Freshly grated Parmesan cheese

1. In a large skillet, warm 1½ tablespoons of the oil over high
heat. Add the garlic, green and red peppers, and rosemary and
quickly sauté, stirring often. Reduce the heat to moderate and
cook until the peppers are soft. Remove the peppers to a bowl,
add the onion, and cook until soft and translucent. Add the onion
to the peppers.
2. Discard the oil in the skillet and wipe it clean with paper towels. Add the remaining 2½ tablespoons oil and bring to the smoking point over high heat. Add the tomato slices and fry very
quickly. Add the basil and *diavoletto* and return the pepper and
onion mixture to the skillet. Season with salt and pepper to taste
and cook over moderately low heat until heated through. Add the
parsley. Set aside but keep warm.
3. In a large pot of salted boiling water, cook the pasta according
to package directions until just *al dente.* Drain well and turn into
a serving bowl.
4. Top the pasta with the sauce and toss. Serve hot, with the Parmesan on the side.

1 bunch fresh broccoli, trimmed and cut into small
  florets
1 pound fusilli, *rotelle,* or *farfalle*
5 garlic cloves
¾ cup olive oil
1 cup loosely packed fresh basil leaves
Pinch of salt
1 large tomato, sliced, or a handful of cherry tomatoes

PASTA DELL'ESTATE
Summer Pasta
Serves 6

1. Blanch the broccoli briefly and drain in a colander.
2. In a large pot of salted boiling water, cook the pasta according
to package directions, until just *al dente.*

3. Meanwhile, in a skillet, combine 3 of the garlic cloves with ¼ cup of oil. Cook over moderate heat until the garlic starts to sizzle. Add the broccoli and stir-fry until tender; do not overcook. Discard the garlic.

4. Drain the pasta, reserving ½ cup of the cooking water. Add the pasta to the skillet and cook, tossing gently with the broccoli over low heat. Remove to a serving bowl.

5. In a food processor or blender, combine the remaining 2 garlic cloves, the remaining ½ cup oil, and the basil and salt. Process until puréed. Add the reserved cooking water and pour the sauce on the pasta-broccoli mixture. Toss and decorate with the tomato before serving.

NOTE: This pasta is usually served at room temperature and is therefore ideal for a party or buffet. Toss again just before serving. Do not chill.

MACCHERONI AI QUATTRO FORMAGGI
Macaroni with Four Cheeses
Serves 4

8 ounces Gruyère cheese
8 ounces Gouda cheese
8 ounces mozzarella cheese
4 tablespoons unsalted butter or ½ cup heavy cream
1 pound macaroni (*penne,* ziti, or rigatoni)
Freshly grated Parmesan cheese

1. Cut the first three cheeses into julienne and set aside.

2. Put the butter or cream in a serving bowl and set aside.

3. In a large pot of salted boiling water, cook the pasta according to package directions, until just *al dente*. Drain, pour into the serving bowl, and toss well. Add the julienne cheeses, two scoops at a time, and toss. Add some of the Parmesan cheese and serve the remainder on the side.

NOTE: The tossing operation should be done quickly and the dish served immediately. The cheese will melt as pasta is being eaten.

1 large head white or purple cauliflower
2 tablespoons unsalted butter
2 tablespoons oil
1 onion, chopped
1 carrot, chopped
2 garlic cloves, minced
1 can (32 ounces) peeled Italian plum tomatoes
5 basil leaves, shredded, or a pinch of dried basil
Pinch of oregano
Pinch of rosemary
Salt and freshly ground pepper
A few flakes of *diavoletto* (Italian hot red pepper flakes, optional)
2 teaspoons coarse (kosher) salt
1 pound macaroni such as ziti, *penne*, or rigatoni

PASTA COL CAVOLFIORE BIANCO O NERO
Pasta with White or Purple Cauliflower
Serves 6

1. Wash and trim the cauliflower; separate it into florets. Cut the tender stems into bite-sized pieces and set aside.

2. In a heatproof casserole, melt the butter in the oil over moderate heat. Add the onion, carrot, and garlic and sauté until the vegetables are tender but not brown, 10 to 15 minutes.

3. Add the tomatoes, herbs, and salt and pepper to taste. Add the *diavoletto* and simmer over low heat for 25 to 30 minutes.

4. Meanwhile, bring a large pot of water to a boil and add 1 teaspoon of the coarse salt. Add the cauliflower and cook for 5 minutes.

5. Remove the cauliflower with a slotted spoon and add it to the tomato sauce. Bring to a boil, reduce the heat to low, and simmer until the vegetables are tender but not mushy. Set aside and keep warm.

6. Bring the water in which the cauliflower cooked to a boil, add the remaining 1 teaspoon coarse salt, and return to a full boil. Add the pasta and cook according to package directions, until *al dente*, stirring occasionally.

7. Drain the pasta and dress with the tomato-cauliflower sauce before serving.

NOTE: This dish can also be served with cheese. I think that Pecorino is best with it.

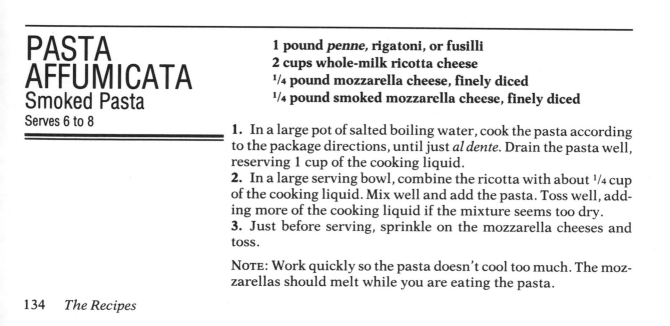

PASTA ALLA SARDA
Sardinian Pasta
Serves 6

1 pound pasta, preferably *penne* or rigatoni
1/2 cup olive oil
1 garlic clove
4 small zucchini (about 1 pound), trimmed and cut into rounds
1/2 cup minced fresh parsley
3 hard-cooked eggs, finely chopped
Salt and freshly ground pepper

1. In a large pot of salted boiling water, cook the pasta according to the package directions, until *al dente*.
2. Meanwhile, in a large skillet, warm the oil over moderate heat. Add the garlic. As soon as the garlic begins to fry, add the zucchini and cook, stirring gently, until tender, about 3 minutes. Add 1/4 cup of the minced parsley and remove from the heat. Stir in the chopped eggs and season to taste with salt and pepper.
3. Drain the pasta and toss it with zucchini mixture. Sprinkle on the remaining 1/4 cup parsley and serve.

PASTA AFFUMICATA
Smoked Pasta
Serves 6 to 8

1 pound *penne*, rigatoni, or fusilli
2 cups whole-milk ricotta cheese
1/4 pound mozzarella cheese, finely diced
1/4 pound smoked mozzarella cheese, finely diced

1. In a large pot of salted boiling water, cook the pasta according to the package directions, until just *al dente*. Drain the pasta well, reserving 1 cup of the cooking liquid.
2. In a large serving bowl, combine the ricotta with about 1/4 cup of the cooking liquid. Mix well and add the pasta. Toss well, adding more of the cooking liquid if the mixture seems too dry.
3. Just before serving, sprinkle on the mozzarella cheeses and toss.

NOTE: Work quickly so the pasta doesn't cool too much. The mozzarellas should melt while you are eating the pasta.

Penne are bias-cut short macaroni. *Coccio* means an earthenware casserole.

  2 tablespoons unsalted butter
  1/2 pound prosciutto or ham, chopped
  1 cup fresh or thawed frozen peas
  2 tablespoons dried mushrooms such as *porcini,* soaked
    in 1/4 cup warm water for 1/2 hour
  1 tablespoon truffle paste (sold in Italian shops,
    optional)
  1 pound *penne*
  1 cup heavy cream
  3/4 cup freshly grated Parmesan cheese
  Freshly ground pepper

1. In a medium heatproof casserole, melt the butter over moderate heat. Add the prosciutto and sauté lightly. Add the peas and stir. Reduce the heat to low, cover, and cook for 3 minutes. (If peas are fresh, add 2 tablespoons water and steam briefly.) Coarsely chop the mushrooms and add them. Cook until the vegetables are tender, adding 1 tablespoon of water if the mixture becomes too dry. Do not overcook.

2. Remove the casserole from the heat, add the truffle paste, and toss; set aside.

3. In a large pot of salted boiling water, cook the *penne* according to the package directions, until *al dente.* Drain and pour the pasta into the casserole; toss gently.

4. Return the casserole to the heat. Stirring constantly over low heat, add the cream. Add the Parmesan a little at a time.

5. When the liquid is almost absorbed and the *penne* are nicely coated with cream, the dish is ready. Serve with additional Parmesan cheese and pass the pepper mill.

NOTE: An enamel casserole can be substituted for an earthenware one.

FUSILLI ALLA FRANCA FALCONE
Franca Falcone's Fusilli
Serves 6

My darling cousin Franca gave me this recipe. It is a favorite of mine, and all my friends seem to love it.

1 can (6 ounces) Italian oil-packed tunafish
1 garlic clove
1 can (8 ounces) tomato sauce
1 pound fusilli
1 tablespoon capers (optional)
20 black olives, pitted and sliced
1/4 chopped fresh parsley

1. Drain the oil from the tuna into a saucepan and add the garlic. Place over low heat and, as soon as the garlic starts to fry, add the tuna. Cook for 2 to 3 minutes, until just heated through. Add the tomato sauce, reduce the heat, and simmer for 20 minutes.
2. Meanwhile, in a large pot of salted boiling water, cook the fusilli according to package directions, until just *al dente*. Drain well and turn into a warm bowl.
3. Add the capers and olives to the sauce and cook for 1 minute, until just heated through. Dress the pasta with the sauce, sprinkle with the parsley, and serve hot.

MACCHERONI ALLA CHITARRA COI FUNGHI
Guitar Macaroni with Mushrooms
Serves 6

1/2 cup dried Italian mushrooms, such as *porcini*, soaked in 1 cup warm water for 1/2 hour
1 garlic clove, peeled
1 onion, chopped
1/4 cup plus 1 tablespoon olive oil
3/4 pound fresh mushrooms, coarsely chopped
Salt
Freshly ground pepper
1 batch homemade noodles, prepared with 6 eggs
4 to 5 sprigs minced fresh parsley
Freshly grated Parmesan cheese (optional)

1. Remove the soaked dried mushrooms from the water, but reserve the soaking water. Coarsely chop the mushrooms and strain the water through a double thickness of dampened cheesecloth into a clean cup. Set both aside.

2. In a large skillet, combine the garlic, onion, and oil over moderate heat. As soon as the garlic begins to fry, add the chopped dried mushrooms and stir in the reserved soaking water. Cook until the water has completely evaporated. Add the fresh mushrooms and salt and pepper to taste. Cover the skillet and cook, stirring occasionally, for 20 to 25 minutes. If too much liquid remains, uncover and let some of it evaporate, but the mixture should not be dry.

3. Meanwhile, in a large pot of salted boiling water, cook the pasta until just *al dente*. Test for doneness as soon as the pasta floats to the top. Drain the pasta, reserving 1 cup of the cooking water, and turn the noodles into a warm serving bowl. Dress with the mushroom sauce, a generous amount of pepper, and the parsley. Toss gently; if too dry, add some of the reserved cooking water. Serve with Parmesan cheese.

MACCHERONI ALLA NORDICA
Nordic Macaroni
Serves 6

1 pound short cut pasta like *penne* or *farfalle*
4 ounces Mascarpone cheese or cream cheese
¹/₂ cup heavy cream
3 tablespoons freshly grated Parmesan cheese
Freshly grated nutmeg
Freshly ground pepper
¹/₄ pound Fontina cheese, cut into julienne strips

1. In a large pot of salted boiling water, cook the pasta according to package directions or until just *al dente*.

2. In a pasta bowl, combine the Mascarpone, cream, Parmesan, and nutmeg and pepper to taste. Beat to a smooth consistency.

3. Drain the pasta, reserving 1 cup of the cooking water. Turn the pasta into the bowl and toss with the sauce. Add some of the cooking water if the pasta seems too dry.

4. Scatter the Fontina over the pasta and toss. Serve immediately, and pass additional Parmesan and pepper if desired.

PENNE ALL' ARRABBIATA
Angry Pasta
Serves 6

This recipe is called Angry Pasta because of the rather pungent taste of the sauce. For a very angry pasta, use quite a bit of *diavoletto*.

3 tablespoons olive oil
1 onion, chopped
1 small carrot, cut into thin rounds
1 can (2 ounces) anchovy fillets, coarsely chopped
1 can (8 ounces) tomato purée
1 pound *penne*
3/4 cup black olives, pitted and sliced
A few flakes of *diavoletto* (Italian hot red pepper flakes, optional)
5 to 6 parsley sprigs, minced

1. In a large skillet, warm the oil over moderate heat. Add the onion and carrot and cook, stirring, until the onion is translucent, about 7 minutes. Add the anchovies and cook for 3 minutes. Stir in the tomato purée and bring to a boil. Reduce the heat to low and simmer, covered, 25 to 30 minutes.
2. Meanwhile, in a large pot of salted boiling water, cook the pasta according to package directions, until just *al dente*. Drain and turn into a serving bowl.
3. Add the olives to the sauce and cook just to heat through. Remove from the heat, add the *diavoletto* and parsley, and dress the pasta with the sauce. Toss well before serving.

Il burino is a Roman bully, a kind of vociferous, ill-mannered person but not totally unlovable.

RIGATONI ALLA BURINA
Bully's Rigatoni
Serves 6

2 tablespoons unsalted butter
1 tablespoon oil
1 onion, finely chopped
1 carrot, finely chopped
1 garlic clove
Salt and freshly ground pepper
1 can (16 ounces) peeled tomatoes
2 teaspoons tomato paste
2 Italian sausages, cut into rounds
½ package thawed frozen peas
1 pound rigatoni
½ cup freshly grated Parmesan and Pecorino Romano cheeses, combined

1. In a large saucepan, melt the butter with the oil over moderate heat. Add the onion, carrot, and garlic and cook, stirring often, until the vegetables begin to brown. Add salt and pepper to taste.

2. Add the peeled tomatoes with their liquid and the tomato paste and cook for 10 minutes. Add the sausages, reduce the heat to low, and cook until the meat is done. Add the peas and cook just to heat through.

3. Preheat the oven to 375°. Butter an ovenproof casserole from which you can serve. In a large pot of salted boiling water, cook the pasta according to package directions, until just *al dente*. Drain the pasta and dress with the sauce, reserving some sauce for the top of the casserole. Add the grated cheeses and toss well. Turn into the prepared casserole, add the remaining sauce, dot with additional butter if desired, and bake until hot and bubbling, 25 to 30 minutes.

TROCCOLI ALLA DAUNIA
Thick Square Noodles Daunia Style
Serves 6 to 8

This is a dish from the cooking of the Daunii, the ancient people inhabiting the region of Apulia. It is a specialty from the excellent Ristorante Ciccolella of Foggia.

About 2½ cups all-purpose flour
2 cups fine semolina flour
5 eggs
4 cups sauce from 1 recipe of Beef Rolls Foggia Style (see page 141), or other sauce
Freshly grated Pecorino Romano or Sardo cheese

1. On a pastry board, combine the flour and the semolina. Make a well in the center and break the eggs into it. Beat the eggs a little with your fingertips. Blend in all the flour, adding a little water if the mixture appears brittle and dry. (This can be done in a large-capacity food processor if desired.) Knead the dough until smooth, adding more flour, a little at a time, if necessary. Cover the dough and set aside to rest for 30 minutes.
2. Roll out the dough ⅛ inch thick and cut through the large cutter of a pasta machine or with a knife. Cut the pasta into 4- to 5-inch pieces, and set aside to dry for a few minutes.
3. In a large pot of salted boiling water, cook the pasta, covered, until just *al dente*, 3 to 4 minutes. Drain, and turn into a serving bowl.
4. Dress with sauce and serve hot with the grated cheese.

1³/₄ **pounds bottom or top round beef, cut into thin slices**
8 ounces Pecorino Romano or Sardo cheese, in one piece
4 ounces *pancetta* **or bacon**
1 tablespoon pine nuts
1 tablespoon raisins
2 garlic cloves, slivered
2 to 3 parsley sprigs, snipped
¹/₄ **cup olive oil**
1 onion, sliced
¹/₂ **cup dry red wine**
1 can (24 ounces) tomato purée or 24 ounces peeled
  tomatoes, strained through a food mill and mixed with
  2 teaspoons tomato paste
Freshly ground pepper

INVOLTINI ALLA FOGGIANA
Beef Rolls Foggia Style
Serves 6 to 8

1. Lightly pound the slices of meat, or ask the butcher to do so.
2. Cut the cheese and the *pancetta* into strips and place an equal amount of each on every slice of meat. Sprinkle the pine nuts, raisins, garlic slivers, and parsley on the meat. Roll each slice and tie with strings.
3. In a casserole, warm the oil over moderate heat. Add the onion and cook until wilted, about 5 minutes. Add the meat rolls and sauté until brown. Add the wine and cook until evaporated.
4. Add the tomato purée and 3 cups of water. Bring to a boil, reduce the heat to low, and simmer, partially covered, for about 2 hours. Stir occasionally, and season to taste with pepper.
5. Use the sauce to dress the *Troccoli alla Daunia* (see page 140). Serve the meat separately.

TIMBALLO DI MACCHERONI ALLA NONNINA
Grandmother's Macaroni Timbale
Serves 8

This recipe was first published in Volume 12 of *The Family Creative Workshop*, Plenary Publications (Tree Communications).

¼ cup unflavored dried bread crumbs
1¼ pounds short macaroni or *penne*
2 eggs, lightly beaten
Bolognese Sauce
2 cups freshly grated Parmesan cheese
1 pound mozzarella cheese, sliced
3 hard-cooked eggs, sliced
4 slices prosciutto, chopped
Tiny Meat Balls
1 cup sliced mushrooms, sautéed in butter
2 tablespoons unsalted butter

1. Butter a 10- to 11-inch ovenproof casserole (or 8 individual ones) and sprinkle with some of the bread crumbs; tap out the excess crumbs. Preheat the oven to 375°.
2. In a large pot of salted boiling water, cook the pasta according to package directions, until just *al dente*. Drain well and return the pasta to the pot. Add the beaten eggs and toss well; let the mixture rest for a few minutes to cook the eggs. Add 3 to 4 ladles of Bolognese Sauce and a handful of Parmesan cheese. Toss gently but thoroughly.
3. In the prepared casserole, place a layer of macaroni or *penne*. Sprinkle with Parmesan cheese and add some of the mozzarella slices, breaking them up if they are too large. Add some of the egg slices, some chopped prosciutto, a few Tiny Meat Balls, and some mushroom slices. Ladle a bit of Bolognese Sauce over this layer. Repeat layering until you have filled the casserole and used all of the mozzarella, egg slices, prosciutto, meat balls, and mushrooms.
4. Top the casserole with the remaining sauce and Parmesan. Lightly sprinkle with the remaining bread crumbs. Dot with the butter and bake for 40 to 45 minutes (less for individual casseroles), until the top looks crusty.
5. Let the *timballo* rest for 15 minutes before slicing it (for individual casseroles, loosen the sides with a knife or spatula, turn upside down, and unmold).

NOTE: The *timballo* can be prepared up to the baking point one day in advance and refrigerated. Reheat, covered, in a 350° oven for 20 minutes.

TINY MEAT BALLS

¹/₂ pound mixed ground beef, veal, and pork
1 teaspoon minced fresh parsley
Pinch of sage
Salt and freshly ground pepper
1 tablespoon unsalted butter

1. In a bowl, combine all of the ingredients except the butter. Wet your hands and make tiny meat balls.
2. In a skillet, melt the butter over moderate heat and sauté the meat balls until browned. Do not overcook.

PASTA CON RAGÙ D'AGNELLO E PEPERONI ALL' ABRUZZESE
Pasta with Lamb and Pepper Ragout Abruzzo Style
Serves 6

Ragù comes from the French *ragoût* and is a kind of stew, usually made with chopped meat.

1/4 cup plus 1 tablespoon olive oil
2 garlic cloves
2 bay leaves
1/2 pound lean lamb, coarsely chopped
1/4 cup dry white wine
1 can (16 ounces) peeled Italian tomatoes, broken up, or
   2 cups Italian tomato purée
2 to 3 red or green bell peppers, cut into thin strips
Salt and freshly ground pepper
1 pound rigatoni or fusilli
Grated Pecorino Romano or Sardo cheese

1. In a heatproof casserole, combine the oil, garlic, and bay leaves over moderate heat. Add the lamb and cook, stirring, until browned. Add the wine and cook until it evaporates.
2. Add the tomatoes, peppers, and salt and pepper to taste. Reduce the heat to low and simmer for 45 minutes to 1 hour. Discard the bay leaves.
3. Shortly before the sauce is finished cooking, cook the pasta in a pot of salted boiling water according to package directions, until just *al dente*. Drain and serve in a bowl, topped with the *ragù*. Place grated cheese in a dish and pass separately.

PASTA DEL FATTORE
Farmer's Pasta
Serves 6

8 very small fresh artichokes (see NOTE)
2 tablespoons olive oil
2 tablespoons unsalted butter
1 small onion, sliced
1/2 cup dry white wine
Freshly ground pepper
1/2 pound whole-milk ricotta cheese
1/4 cup milk
1/4 cup plus 1 tablespoon freshly grated Parmesan cheese
2 egg yolks
1 pound short pasta such as rigatoni, *penne,* or fusilli
3 to 4 parsley sprigs, minced

1. Trim the artichokes by removing the outer leaves and trimming away about $1/2$ inch from the points of the other leaves. Drop the artichokes into a bowl of water to which lemon juice has been added in order to prevent discoloration.

2. In a pot of boiling water, blanch the artichokes for a few minutes. When cool enough to handle, cut into quarters.

3. In a medium saucepan, warm the oil and butter over moderate heat. Add the onion and sauté until translucent, about 5 minutes. Add the artichokes and cook for 3 minutes. Add the wine and pepper to taste. Cook slowly until the artichokes are tender, 15 to 20 minutes.

4. In a large serving bowl, combine the ricotta with the milk. Stir until the ricotta is creamy and smooth, adding an additional tablespoon or two of milk, if necessary.

5. In a small bowl, beat the Parmesan and egg yolks. Add to the ricotta mixture, along with the artichoke-onion mixture, and stir. Set aside and keep warm.

6. In a large pot of salted boiling water, cook the pasta according to package directions, until just *al dente*. Drain well and add to the ricotta mixture. Toss, sprinkle with the parsley, and serve at once.

NOTE: Thawed frozen artichoke hearts can be used for this recipe. Add them to the onion and cook over high heat for 5 to 6 minutes.

This dish is quite popular in the Veneto region of Italy and a specialty of the city of Padua, where I grew up.

> 1 can (2 ounces) anchovy fillets
> Olive oil
> 1 large onion, chopped
> $1/4$ cup dry white wine
> 1 cup California ripe olives, pitted and sliced

BIGOLI IN SALSA D'ACCIUGHE
Whole-Wheat Pasta with Anchovy Sauce
Serves 6

1 tablespoon capers, chopped
4 to 5 parsley sprigs, minced
1 batch whole-wheat *bigoli* (see NOTE) made with 4 eggs
Coarse (kosher) salt
Freshly ground pepper

1. Drain the oil from the anchovies into a measuring cup. Add olive oil to measure $1/4$ cup. Pour the oil into a large saucepan and add the onion. Cook, covered, over low heat until the onion is soft, 30 to 40 minutes, stirring occasionally. Add the wine, increase the heat to moderate, and cook until the wine evaporates.
2. Coarsely chop the anchovies. Add to the onion mixture and cook for 3 minutes. Add the olives and capers and cook just to heat through. Stir in half of the parsley.
3. In a large pot of salted boiling water, cook the *bigoli*. As soon as the pasta floats to the surface, add 1 cup of cold water to stop the cooking. Drain the pasta, reserving 1 cup of the water.
4. Pour the *bigoli* into a serving bowl and dress with the anchovy sauce. If the mixture looks too dry, add some of the reserved water. Sprinkle on the remaining parsley and pass the pepper mill at the table.

NOTE: *Bigoli* are a type of round spaghetti extruded through a special pasta machine. To make them at home, roll out the dough a little thicker than you would for noodles and put through the narrow cutters of a hand-cranked pasta machine.

TIMBALLO DI ZITONI ALL'IMPIEDI
Standing Ziti Timbale
Serves 6

To assemble this dish, you need all your hands, elbows, and knees. However, a pupil of mine devised a very simple method of keeping the *zitoni* standing. Twist some foil into a ring and set it in the baking dish. You can then stand *zitoni* around the sides of the pan between the walls and the foil ring.

1 pound *zitoni* (big ziti)
7 tablespoons unsalted butter

6 tablespoons freshly grated Parmesan cheese

**³/₄ pound mozzarella cheese, cut into strips the same
length as the ziti**

**¹/₂ pound prosciutto, cut into strips the same length as
the ziti**

¹/₄ cup all-purpose flour

2 cups milk

6 eggs, separated

3 tablespoons grated smoked mozzarella cheese

2 to 3 parsley sprigs, minced

Salt and freshly ground pepper

1. Preheat the oven to 350°. Butter a round ovenproof casserole or soufflé dish that will hold the *zitoni* when standing. In a large pot of salted boiling water, cook the *zitoni* according to package directions, until just *al dente*. Drain and turn the pasta into a bowl. Add 4 tablespoons of the butter and 2 tablespoons of the Parmesan and toss. With foil ring in place, stand the *zitoni* all around the circumference of the baking dish. Alternating strips of mozzarella with strips of prosciutto, make a circle of these ingredients inside the circle of pasta. Add a second circle of pasta and continue making concentric circles until all of the pasta, mozzarella, and prosciutto is used up. There might be a 3- to 4-inch empty space in the center of the dish; if not, do not worry.

2. In a medium saucepan, melt the remaining 3 tablespoons of butter over moderate heat and add the flour. Cook, whisking, for 3 minutes. Off the heat, slowly add some of the milk, stirring and "melting" the sauce. Continue adding the remaining milk until the mixture is liquid and smooth.

3. Return the saucepan to moderate heat and cook, stirring constantly, until the sauce starts to "puff." Remove it from the heat and cool.

4. One at a time, add the egg yolks to the sauce, stirring between additions. Add the remaining 4 tablespoons Parmesan, the smoked mozzarella, parsley, and salt and pepper to taste.

5. In a bowl, beat the egg whites until stiff. Gently fold the whites into the sauce.

6. Spoon the sauce over the pasta, taking care that some of it goes into the tubes of the pasta. If there is a space in the center of the dish, spoon any remaining sauce into the space. Bake for about 1 hour, until the top is nicely colored.

7. Let stand for about 10 minutes before serving.

Standing Ziti Timbale

CANNELLONI ALLA ANNA TERESA

Anna Teresa's Cannelloni

Serves 6

This is my signature recipe. It was first published in *The Family Creative Workshop* series, Volume 12, Plenary Publications for Time-Life. I also made this dish during the showing of my own TV documentary, "Let Them Eat Pasta!", produced by *Camera Three* for CBS. The documentary was rebroadcast on PBS nationwide.

STUFFING

NOTE: If you are entertaining, the stuffing can be prepared a day in advance.

1 pound whole-milk ricotta cheese
1 Italian *salamino* or 1 dry sausage, chopped fine
½ pound fresh spinach or ½ package frozen spinach, cooked, squeezed, and sautéed briefly in a little butter and finely chopped
Salt and freshly ground pepper to taste
4 ounces Gruyère cheese, chopped
1 egg, beaten
Pinch of freshly grated nutmeg
½ cup freshly grated Parmesan cheese

PASTA AND SAUCE

4 cups Sugo di Carne (meat sauce, see page 39)
1 batch homemade pasta dough prepared with 4 eggs
Coarse (kosher) salt

1. In a large bowl, combine all of the stuffing ingredients. Add one or two ladlefuls of the meat sauce and mix well. Taste for flavoring and set aside. (The stuffing can be prepared one day in advance.)
2. Roll the pasta dough through a pasta machine until rather thin. Cut the strips of dough into 6-inch lengths and set aside to dry.
3. Choose two baking dishes from which you can serve that are large enough to contain all cannelloni in one layer. Butter the dishes and pour a thin layer of sauce into the bottom of each dish. Set aside.

4. Preheat the oven to 375°. In a medium, not too tall casserole or saucepan, bring water to a boil. Add a handful of coarse salt and cook 4 to 5 pieces of dough at a time until they float to the surface. Drain the sheets of dough flat on a dampened linen cloth.
5. While the remaining dough cooks, start filling the cannelloni. Place 1 tablespoon of the stuffing mixture on one end of each piece of drained dough. Roll into a tube and place, seam side down in the prepared baking dishes. Continue until all of the cannelloni are filled.
6. Pour the remaining meat sauce over the cannelloni, but do not drown them. Sprinkle with additional Parmesan and dot with butter if desired. Bake until hot and bubbly, about 30 to 35 minutes.

STUFFING FOR RAVIOLI OR CANNELLONI ALLA ANNA TERESA

To fill about 200 ravioli or 36 cannelloni

1 pound ricotta cheese
1 Italian *salamino* or 1 dry sausage, finely chopped
1 pound fresh spinach or 1 package (10-ounce) frozen spinach, cooked, squeezed dry, sautéed briefly in a little butter, and finely chopped
Salt and freshly ground pepper
8 ounces Gruyère cheese, chopped
1 egg, beaten
Pinch of freshly grated nutmeg
Freshly grated Parmesan cheese

1. In a bowl, combine all of the ingredients and mix well.
2. Wrap tightly in plastic or foil and refrigerate. This stuffing can be prepared a day ahead of time.

NOTE: If you are dressing the ravioli or cannelloni with a meat sauce or a tomato sauce, add some of the sauce to the stuffing.

RAVIOLI DI RICOTTA
Ricotta-Stuffed Ravioli
Serves 6 to 8

1 batch homemade pasta dough made with 4 eggs
½ batch Stuffing for Cannelloni alla Anna Teresa (page 149)
2 cups homemade *ragù* sauce (page 40)
Freshly grated Parmesan cheese

1. Cut the dough into wedges and roll the wedges, one at a time, through a pasta machine into thin sheets. Place one sheet of dough over a ravioli tray and gently press the dough into the depressions. Place a small amount of filling in each depression. Dip a finger into a glass of water and run it along the lines where the ravioli will be cut. Cover the filled squares with another sheet of dough, pressing down along the dampened edges to seal the two sheets. Roll a rolling pin over the tray, cutting and sealing the ravioli completely. Turn the tray over and gently separate the ravioli. Repeat until all of the dough is used.
2. Bring a large pot of water to a boil and add a good handful of salt. Add the ravioli and cook for a few minutes, until just *al dente*. Drain and dress with the sauce. Serve hot with a bowl of Parmesan cheese on the side.

NOTE: Ravioli can also be dressed with butter and Parmesan or with cream and Parmesan. If using cream, set the dressed pasta in a 375° oven for about 15 minutes, until the cream is thickened.

CANNELLONI ALL'ETRUSCA
Cannelloni with Mushrooms, Ham, and Cheese
Serves 6 to 8

The Etruscans lived in Italy during the fourth and fifth centuries B.C. They were a highly civilized people, great architects and makers of tools which today are still used. Their tombs were filled with domestic utensils, including the instruments for making pasta. This was many centuries before Marco Polo's adventurous voyage. As you can see, he didn't have to bring spaghetti back to Italy!

2 tablespoons unsalted butter
1 pound fresh mushrooms, coarsely chopped
Salt and freshly ground pepper
2 tablespoons dried mushrooms, soaked ¹/₂ hour in ¹/₄
   cup warm water
3 cups Béchamel Sauce (see page 42)
1 batch homemade pasta dough prepared with 4 eggs
¹/₄ pound Gruyère cheese, shredded
¹/₄ cup chopped prosciutto
¹/₄ cup heavy cream
Freshly grated Parmesan cheese

1. In a large skillet, melt the butter over moderate heat. Add the fresh mushrooms and sauté until soft and limp, about 20 minutes. Season to taste with salt and pepper. With a slotted spoon, remove the mushrooms to a bowl and set aside.

2. Drain the dried mushrooms and reserve the liquid. Chop the mushrooms coarsely and sauté in whatever butter remains in the skillet. Cook until the mushrooms give up and then absorb their liquid. Add the mushrooms to the other mushrooms. Stir in 2 cups of the béchamel and set aside.

3. Roll out the pasta dough into thin sheets. Using a fluted wheel, cut out 6 × 5-inch rectangles.

4. In a large pot of salted boiling water, cook four or five of the rectangles of dough at a time until they float to the top. Drain and arrange flat on dampened tea towels. Spoon 2 tablespoons of the mushroom mixture in the center of each rectangle and roll into a tube shape to enclose the filling.

5. Butter a large baking pan and line it with a single layer of the cannelloni. Strain the reserved mushroom liquid through a double thickness of dampened cheesecloth and add the liquid to the remaining béchamel. Mix and pour over the cannelloni. Scatter the top evenly with the Gruyère and prosciutto. Pour on the heavy cream and top with a sprinkling of Parmesan. Bake the cannelloni until bubbly and slightly colored, about 30 minutes.

TORTELLINI DELL'ESTATE
Summer Tortellini
Serves 6

I like to make the stuffing for this dish a day ahead of time.

STUFFING

¹/₂ boneless chicken breast
1 tablespoon unsalted butter
1 tablespoon olive oil
Salt and freshly ground pepper
Pinch of sage
2 tablespoons chopped mortadella
1 small egg, lightly beaten
Freshly grated nutmeg

PASTA AND SAUCE

1 batch homemade spinach dough prepared with 4 eggs
8 ounces mozzarella cheese (preferably made from
  buffalo's milk), diced
8 to 9 plum tomatoes, peeled, seeded, and chopped
1 cup pitted black olives, sliced into rounds
¹/₄ cup olive oil
Pinch of oregano
5 to 6 fresh basil leaves or pinch of dried
Salt and freshly ground pepper

1. Prepare the stuffing: Cube the chicken. In a skillet, melt the butter and oil together over moderate heat. Add the chicken and sauté, but do not overcook.
2. In a food processor, combine the chicken and all remaining stuffing ingredients and chop very fine. Set aside.
3. Make the tortellini: Roll the dough into very thin sheets. Using a tortellini cutter or a small glass, cut the dough into rounds and set aside.
4. Put a small amount of stuffing in the center of each round. Dip a finger in water and moisten the edge of the round. Fold into a half-moon and press to seal the edges. Pick up the half-moon and pinch the two pointed ends together, forming a little peaked cap-shaped dumpling.
5. Cook the pasta: To a large pot of salted boiling water, add the

tortellini. Stir, cover, and let the water come back to a boil again. If the tortellini are fresh, they are done as soon as they float on the surface. Taste to make sure they are done to your taste.

6. Drain the tortellini and turn into a serving bowl. Add the mozzarella, tomatoes, olives, oil, oregano, basil, and salt and pepper to taste. Toss until the mozzarella melts and serve at room temperature. If you wish to refrigerate leftovers, let the dish come to room temperature again before serving.

NOTE: This quantity makes about 160 tortellini.

TORTELLINI TARTUFFATI ALLA PANNA
Truffled Tortellini with Cream
Serves 6

¹/₂ boneless skinless chicken breast (about ¹/₂ pound)
1 tablespoon unsalted butter
1 tablespoon olive oil
2 tablespoons chopped prosciutto or mortadella
1 egg, lightly beaten
Freshly grated nutmeg
Pinch of sage
Salt and freshly ground pepper
1 batch homemade pasta dough, prepared with 2 eggs
1 tablespoon truffle paste
1 cup heavy cream
Freshly grated Parmesan cheese

1. Cube the chicken. In a large skillet, melt the butter with the oil. Sauté the chicken, but do not overcook. In a food processor, combine the chicken, prosciutto, egg, nutmeg, sage, and salt and pepper to taste. Process until chopped very fine.

2. Roll the pasta dough into very thin sheets. Using a tortellini cutter or a glass, cut rounds and set aside. Gather the scraps, roll them out, and cut more rounds.

3. Put a scant teaspoon of the stuffing in the center of each round. Dip your finger in a glass of water and run it around the edge of the circle. Fold the circle in half and press the edges to seal. Pick up the half circle and pinch the two pointed ends together, forming a little peaked-cap shape. Continue until all of the dough and stuffing is used.

4. Preheat oven to 350°. In a large pot of salted boiling water, cook the tortellini until they float to the top. Butter a standard-size soufflé dish. Drain the pasta and place in the buttered dish.

5. In a small bowl, combine the truffle paste and just enough cream to liquefy the paste. Pour the remaining cream and the truffle mixture over the tortellini. Sprinkle with Parmesan cheese and bake for about 30 minutes.

NOTE: This quantity of dough makes about 130 tortellini.

TORTELLINI CON LA SALSA DI FEGATO D'OCA
Tortellini in Goose Liver Sauce
Serves 6

The first time I went to the famosissimo restaurant in San Domenico of Imola, Mr. Morini, the owner, played the exquisite host, as he does with all his clients. But he didn't let me choose my meal; he decided for me, and I was delighted. One dish, though, I would not have ordered, the tortellini in a goose liver sauce—I am not all that fond of liver (although I adore pâté). However, relying on Gianluigi Morini's impeccable taste, I didn't refuse it. I'm so pleased—what a mistake I would have made! Here is the recipe for you to judge.

2 tablespoons olive oil
1¹/₂ pounds pork chops, cubed, with the bone included
1 boneless chicken breast (about ¹/₂ pound), cubed
4 ounces prosciutto, chopped
3 eggs

¾ cup freshly grated Parmesan cheese
Salt and freshly ground pepper
Pinch of freshly grated nutmeg
1 batch fresh homemade pasta made with 2 eggs
1½ cups heavy cream
6 to 8 ounces goose liver pâté (see NOTE)
4 tablespoons butter
Freshly grated Parmesan cheese, for serving

1. In a skillet, warm the oil over moderate heat. Add the pork and cook until the meat loses its pinkness. Add the chicken and sauté until both meats are thoroughly cooked. Stir in the prosciutto during the last 2 to 3 minutes.
2. Remove the pork bones and discard them. Turn the meats into the bowl of a food processor, and add the egg and ¾ cup Parmesan. Process briefly; the mixture should have texture. Season to taste with salt and pepper and nutmeg and set the filling aside.
3. Roll out the pasta into a thin sheet and cut, with a tortellini cutter or a small glass, into 2-inch circles. Do not let the pasta dry. Place a tiny amount of filling on each circle, moisten the edges all around, and fold in half. Pick up the half-moon-shaped dumpling and fold to pinch the two pointed corners together. Repeat until you use all of the pasta. Set a kitchen towel on a large tray and place the tortellini on it.
4. In a food processor, combine the cream with a few pieces of the liver pâté. Process, adding the remaining pieces of liver, until the sauce is a very smooth consistency.
5. In a large pot of salted boiling water, cook the fresh tortellini until they float to the top. If you use dried tortellini, cook a little longer. Drain.
6. Place the pasta in a serving bowl and add the butter. Toss gently. Warm the sauce if it has cooled and dress the tortellini. Toss again and serve with the Parmesan cheese.

NOTE: The amount of liver used in the sauce is according to your taste; you can use less or add more.

ZUPPA DI VERDURE ALLA GENOVESE
Genoa-Style Vegetable Soup
Serves 6

1 tablespoon olive oil
1 large onion, sliced
2 to 3 parsley sprigs, minced
3 potatoes, peeled and diced
2 to 3 carrots, scraped and diced
3 to 4 celery ribs with leaves, cut into small pieces
1 Savoy cabbage or 1 bunch escarole or endive, shredded
2 zucchini, diced
3/4 cup small pasta such as *tubetti* or *orzo*
2 firm ripe tomatoes, peeled, seeded, and coarsely
  chopped
1 garlic clove, minced
1 to 2 tablespoons chopped fresh basil
1 slice bacon, minced (optional)
Salt
Freshly grated Parmesan cheese

1. In a large heatproof casserole, warm the oil over moderate heat. Add the onion and cook until translucent. Do not allow the onion to color. Add the parsley and cook briefly, about 1 minute. Add the potatoes and carrots and cook, stirring, for 2 minutes. Add 2 cups water and cook for 20 minutes.
2. Add the celery and cabbage and cook for 3 minutes. Add 4 cups of water and simmer for 30 minutes, until the potatoes are cooked.
3. Add the zucchini and pasta and cook for 5 minutes. Stir in the tomatoes and cook for 5 minutes. Add the garlic, basil, bacon, and salt to taste. Simmer for 1 minute and remove from the heat.
4. Serve. Pass the freshly grated Parmesan cheese on the side.

NOTE: If you like, this minestrone can be served lukewarm or at room temperature (omit the Parmesan). It also freezes and reheats well.

Bruno Creglia, who with his brother Lucio owns the winsome New York restaurant Giordano, sent me this recipe. I once had confessed to him that my gnocchi were seldom as perfectly textured as his. The letter attached to the recipe read, "As promised I am sending you the recipe for the gnocchi and I wish you a good result. If not, you have only one solution: Present yourself at the door of my restaurant at 7 A.M. [good heavens, for me it is still dawn] and start practicing with my chef." I didn't need to go; this recipe works perfectly.

GNOCCHI ALLA GIORDANO
Gnocchi Giordano Style
Serves 6 to 8

> 2 pounds baking potatoes
> 1 cup sifted all-purpose flour
> 1 whole egg plus 1 egg yolk, lightly beaten together
> 2 tablespoons unsalted butter, softened
> 1 teaspoon salt
> Freshly grated Parmesan cheese

1. Boil the potatoes in their jackets until cooked through. Drain, and put through a ricer or food mill. While the potatoes are still warm, blend in the flour. Add the egg, egg yolk, butter, and salt.
2. Place the potato mixture on a floured board and knead lightly; the dough will be soft. Roll the dough into 1 inch thick sticks about 10 inches long. Cut each roll into ¾-inch pieces.
3. Rub each piece of dough over a medium grater to give it the desired shape. In a large pot of salted boiling water, cook the gnocchi until they rise to the top of the water. Using a slotted spoon, remove the gnocchi to a warm bowl. Sprinkle with Parmesan cheese and additional butter. Serve at once, topped with one of your favorite sauces.

GNOCCHI DI PATATE TRICOLORE
Tricolored Potato Gnocchi
Serves 6

2 pounds potatoes
1 egg, lightly beaten
2 cups all-purpose flour
1 small red beet, boiled, peeled, and mashed
1/2 cup cooked spinach, squeezed dry and finely chopped
1 1/2 cups Sugo Finto sauce (see page 36)
Freshly grated Parmesan cheese

1. In a saucepan, boil the potatoes until tender. Peel them and mash.

2. Turn the mashed potato onto a pastry board and make a well in the center. Add the egg and mix with the potato. Start adding the flour while kneading into a smooth, soft dough. (Some potatoes will absorb more flour than others. You might need slightly more or less than 2 cups of flour.)

3. Divide the dough into 3 equal parts. Knead the beet purée into one of the parts and the chopped spinach into another. Set the third ball of dough aside.

4. To make the gnocchi: Break off a small amount of dough at a time and shape into a thin, cigar-shaped strip. Cut into 1-inch pieces. Gently press each piece on the tines of a fork or on a grater to shape it. Place the gnocchi on floured linen napkins to dry a bit. (Napkins are essential to absorb the humidity of the potatoes.)

5. In a large pot of salted boiling water, cook the gnocchi in batches for about 3 to 5 minutes. Drain, place in a serving bowl, and dress with sauce and cheese. Keep warm in a low oven while cooking the remaining gnocchi. The gnocchi should "sit" in the sauce for about 10 minutes before serving.

NOTE: Another simple way to dress gnocchi is in butter and Parmesan, to which you may add a little cream.

4 cups (1 quart) milk
1½ cups semolina (farina)
1 egg
½ pound (2 sticks) unsalted butter, at room temperature
Freshly grated Parmesan cheese
Salt

GNOCCHI DI SEMOLINA ALLA ROMANA
Roman-Style Semolina Gnocchi
Serves 6

1. In a saucepan, bring the milk to a boil over moderately high heat. Pour in the semolina in a steady stream, stirring all the time to prevent lumps. Reduce the heat to low and cook, stirring constantly, until the mixture is very thick, about 5 minutes.

2. Remove the semolina from the heat, add the egg, ¼ pound of the butter, a good handful of Parmesan cheese, and salt to taste. Stir to combine well.

3. Lightly moisten a marble slab or an uncoated cookie sheet. Pour the semolina mixture on it. Wet a large spatula and flatten the mixture to a 1-inch thickness. Refrigerate until firm, about 1 hour.

4. Butter an ovenproof dish. Preheat the oven to 375°. Cut the semolina into diamonds or rounds and arrange one layer in the buttered dish. Sprinkle with Parmesan and dot with butter. Continue layering, starting each layer a little way in from the layer below it so that the layers of gnocchi will form a pyramid shape. Sprinkle each layer with Parmesan cheese and dot with butter. Top with the remaining butter and cheese. Bake until the top is nicely colored, 25 to 30 minutes.

CHICCHE VERDI DEL NONNO
Grandpa's Green Dumplings
Serves 4

These green gnocchi were a favorite of Giuseppe Verdi, the *"nonno"* for whom this recipe from Carlo Bergonzi's restaurant in Busseto, I Due Foscari, is named. Carlo's charming son Marco gave me the recipe during a delicious repast at their restaurant, which Marco directs.

CHICCHE

1¹/₂ pounds potatoes, boiled, peeled, and puréed
3 cups all-purpose flour
¹/₂ pound spinach, washed, cooked, squeezed dry, and
    very finely chopped
2 eggs
Pinch of salt

CREAM SAUCE

8 tablespoons (1 stick) unsalted butter
1 tablespoon tomato paste
¹/₂ cup heavy cream
Pinch of salt
Freshly grated Parmesan cheese

1. Make the *chicche*: Combine all the *chicche* ingredients except a bit of the flour, and work into a smooth and pliable dough, well dusted with the extra flour.
2. Roll the dough into cylinders about ¹/₂ inch in diameter and slice into pieces about ³/₄ inch long.
3. Bring 5 quarts or more of salted water to a boil, and drop in the *chicche*. When all have risen to the surface, let them boil a few seconds more. Add cold water and drain.
4. Make the sauce: In a large saucepan, melt the butter over low heat. Stir in the tomato paste. Add the cream, and stir until the sauce is smooth. Add salt to taste.
5. Add the drained *chicche*, and toss over moderate heat until hot and well coated with the sauce. Add plenty of grated Parmesan, transfer to a warm platter, and serve.

DOUGH

About 2½ cups all-purpose flour
1½ cups semolina flour
Pinch of salt

SAUCE

1 can (16 ounces) peeled tomatoes or 1 pound fresh ripe
  plum tomatoes
1 or 2 garlic cloves, peeled
4 to 5 basil leaves or ¼ teaspoon dried basil
¼ plus 1 tablespoon olive oil
Salt and freshly ground pepper
3 bunches of arugula, washed, trimmed, and leaves cut
  in half
Freshly grated Pecorino Romano cheese

CAVATELLI CON L'ARUGOLA
Little Dumplings with Arugula
Serves 6

1. Make the dough: On a pastry board, combine the flour and semolina. Make a well in the center.
2. Add a pinch of salt to 1 cup of lukewarm water and pour some of it in the well. Blend the flour and the water, adding more water if necessary to obtain a rather stiff dough. Knead until smooth and elastic. Cover with a bowl, and let the dough rest for 20 minutes.
3. Make the sauce: In a saucepan, combine the tomatoes, garlic, basil, oil, and salt and pepper to taste. Bring to a boil, reduce the heat to low, and simmer for 15 to 20 minutes.
4. Break off pieces of dough and roll into cylinders the size and shape of cigars. Cut into ½-inch pieces and, pushing with the thumb, form each piece into a little shell-like dumpling. Let dry on trays covered with tea towels.
5. In a large pot of salted boiling water, cook the arugula for 10 minutes and add the *cavatelli*. Cook until just *al dente*, drain, and dress with the sauce.
6. Serve hot and pass the Romano cheese.

Salads

1 bunch arugula, washed and trimmed
2 heads Belgian endive
2 tablespoons olive oil
Juice of ½ lemon or 2 tablespoons red wine vinegar
Freshly ground pepper

1. Tear the arugula into bite-sized pieces. Cut the endive into ½-inch rounds. Combine the greens in a salad bowl.
2. In a jar, shake together the oil and lemon juice. Pour over the salad and toss just before serving. Add a sprinkling of pepper to each portion.

INSALATA DI ARUGOLA E INDIVIA BELGA
Arugula and Belgian Endive Salad
Serves 6

ASPARAGI AL LIMONE
Asparagus with Lemon
Serves 6

This dish can be served as an antipasto or a salad.

1½ pounds asparagus, trimmed and stems peeled
Olive oil
Lemon wedges

1. Cook the asparagus in boiling water or steam until each spear bends a little but does not get limp. Do not overcook. Refresh under cold water, drain, and wrap in paper towels. Let cool.
2. Arrange the asparagus on individual dishes. Drizzle olive oil over and serve with lemon wedges.

INSALATA ROSATA DI FAGIOLINI
Beet and String Bean Salad
Serves 6

1 pound string beans, steamed
2 red beets, boiled
1 garlic clove, minced
1 teaspoon grainy mustard
¼ cup olive oil
2 tablespoons red wine vinegar

1. Cut the string beans into bite-sized pieces and set aside. Slice the beets and set aside.
2. In a serving bowl, combine the garlic, mustard, oil, and vinegar. Add the string beans and toss well. Arrange the beets around the edge of the bowl, but *do not toss* until ready to serve.

1 bunch arugula, washed and trimmed
2 red beets, boiled and peeled
¹/₄ cup olive oil
1¹/₂ tablespoons red wine vinegar
Freshly ground pepper

1. In a salad bowl, break the arugula into bite-sized pieces. Slice the beets and arrange them in the middle or around the sides of the bowl.
2. In a small bowl, whisk together the oil, vinegar, and a pinch of pepper. Mix vigorously and pour over the salad. Toss just before serving.

INSALATA DI RAPE ROSSE ED ARUGOLA
Red Beet and Arugula Salad
Serves 6

---

1 bunch broccoli, cut into florets, stems peeled, cut on the bias, and blanched
1 cup cherry tomatoes
¹/₄ pound mild Gorgonzola cheese
¹/₄ cup olive oil
2 tablespoons lemon juice
1 cucumber, peeled and thinly sliced

1. Place the broccoli florets and stems and the tomatoes in a large salad bowl.
2. In a small bowl, crumble the Gorgonzola. Add the oil and lemon juice and mix. Pour the dressing over the broccoli and tomatoes. Arrange the cucumber slices in a decorative fashion and toss just before serving.

NOTE: This dressing is very good on cucumbers alone. I like to add a few chopped mint leaves to it as well.

INSALATA DI BROCCOLI, POMODORI, E CETRIOLI AL GORGONZOLA
Broccoli, Tomato, and Cucumber Salad with Gorgonzola
Serves 6

MELANZANE ALLA BARESE
Bari-Style Eggplant
Serves 6

An earthy recipe from Bari, the capital city of Apulia in the south of Italy.

2 to 3 medium eggplants (about 2 pounds)
Coarse (kosher) salt
2 garlic cloves
4 parsley sprigs
4 basil leaves
4 mint leaves
$1/4$ cup olive oil
Freshly ground pepper

1. Cut the unpeeled eggplants lengthwise into $1/4$-inch slices. Place the slices in a bowl, sprinkle generously with coarse salt, and add water to cover. Set aside for 30 minutes.

2. Drain the eggplants and pat the slices dry with paper towels. Working in batches, arrange the slices on a broiler pan and broil until lightly browned, about 2 minutes per side. Set aside.

3. In a food processor or blender, combine the garlic, parsley, basil, mint, and olive oil. Process briefly until the mixture becomes a purée. Season to taste with pepper.

4. Line a serving dish with a layer of eggplant slices. Drizzle lightly with some of the purée. Continue adding layers and sauce until the ingredients are used. Set aside, covered, for at least 2 hours. Serve at room temperature. (If you make this dish ahead of time, cover tightly with plastic or foil and refrigerate. Be sure to allow the dish to come to room temperature before serving.)

NOTE: Bay leaves can be substituted for the mint. However, do not purée them; add them whole to each layer.

1½ cups cooked beans, preferably red or black
1½ cups cooked chick-peas
1 small red onion, coarsely chopped
4 to 5 tablespoons olive oil
2 tablespoons red wine vinegar
1 teaspoon grainy mustard

INSALATA DI DUE FAGIOLI
Two-Bean Salad
Serves 6

1. In a bowl, combine the beans, chick-peas, and onion. Add 4 tablespoons of the oil, the vinegar, and mustard, and mix well. If the mixture seems too dry, add the remaining 1 tablespoon oil. Toss well and set aside for several hours to allow the flavors to mingle.
2. Toss again before serving.

NOTE: This salad improves if it sets for a few days. It will keep for up to one week.

1 large cauliflower
1 cup mayonnaise (see page 41)
1 tablespoon grainy mustard

INSALATA DI CAVOLFIORI
Cauliflower Salad
Serves 6

1. Break the cauliflower into florets, cut the stems into sticks, and chill.
2. Before serving, arrange the cauliflower florets in a bowl. Combine the mayonnaise and mustard and pour over the cauliflower.

NOTE: You can serve cauliflower as an antipasto with drinks. Place the florets in a basket. Set a bowl with mustard-mayonnaise in the middle and use as a dip.

MELANZANE MEDITERRANEE
Mediterranean Eggplant
Serves 2 to 3

For a really indigenous flavor, the eggplants should be roasted over a flame. The end result is worth the bother.

2 medium eggplants
1/4 cup olive oil
1 garlic clove, mashed
1/2 teaspoon Dijon-style mustard
Juice of 1/2 lemon
1 teaspoon capers, minced
1 tablespoon minced fresh parsley

1. With a fork, pierce the eggplants in 2 or 3 places and roast over a flame or under an electric broiler, turning often, until the skin is charred. Or, without piercing the skin, bake in a 375° oven until the vegetables "collapse."
2. Peel and cube the eggplants, removing the seeds, if possible.
3. Place the eggplant in a serving dish. In a bowl, combine all of the other ingredients and pour over the eggplant. Toss and serve at room temperature.

NOTE: This mixture can be mashed or puréed and served as a spread or dip. In either case, a basket of warm pita bread wedges is an ideal accompaniment.

INSALATA DI FAGIOLINI MIMOSA
String Bean Salad Mimosa
Serves 8

1/4 cup olive oil
1 garlic clove, minced
1/2 teaspoon grainy mustard
1 tablespoon red wine vinegar or 2 tablespoons lemon
   juice
2 pounds string beans, blanched
1 hard-cooked egg

1. In a serving bowl, combine the oil, garlic, mustard, and vinegar; mix well. Add the string beans and toss.
2. Separate the egg yolk from the white and coarsely chop each of them. Sprinkle the yolk in the center of the beans and encircle with the chopped egg white. Toss just before serving.

1 pound string beans, trimmed and washed
3 tablespoons olive oil
Juice of ½ lemon

INSALATA SEMPLICE DI FAGIOLINI
Simple String Bean Salad
Serves 6

1. Plunge the string beans into boiling water. Cook until tender, 6 to 8 minutes. Refresh the beans under cold water; drain and refrigerate.
2. When cool, cut the beans into bite-sized pieces and dress with the oil and lemon.

6 firm plum tomatoes, sliced
4 Kirby cucumbers, thinly sliced
1 garlic clove, minced
¼ cup olive oil
2 tablespoons red wine vinegar
Freshly ground pepper
Pinch of basil or minced fresh basil leaves

INSALATA DI POMODORI E CETRIOLI
Tomato and Cucumber Salad
Serves 6

1. In a serving bowl or dish, arrange the tomato and cucumber slices in a decorative fashion.
2. In a small bowl, combine the garlic, oil, vinegar, pepper, and basil. Whisk to blend well and pour on the prepared vegetables.

1 pound mozzarella cheese, sliced
2 to 3 firm ripe tomatoes, sliced
Olive oil
Fresh basil leaves

LA CAPRESE
Capri-Style Salad
Serves 6

On a serving dish, arrange the mozzarella and tomato slices in alternate rows. Drizzle with the olive oil and tuck the basil leaves between some of the slices.

NOTE: This dish can be served as an antipasto or a salad.

INSALATA DI ZUCCHINE
Zucchini Salad
Serves 6 to 8

1 pound zucchini, blanched
2 green and 2 red bell peppers, roasted (see page 33)
3 tomatoes
1 medium red onion
1/2 cup black olives, pitted (optional)

DRESSING

5 tablespoons olive oil
Juice of 1 lemon
1 scant teaspoon grainy mustard
1 parsley sprig, minced
Pinch of cumin
Freshly ground pepper
1 garlic clove, minced

1. Cut the zucchini into thin rounds. Peel the roasted peppers and cut into strips. Slice the tomatoes. Place in a salad bowl or arrange on a serving dish.
2. Cut the onion into rings and scatter over the vegetables. Decorate with the olives. Cover with dampened paper towels and chill.
3. When ready to serve, combine all of the dressing ingredients and pour over the salad. Toss well and serve.

INSALATA ALLA SIRACUSANA
Siracusa-Style Salad
Serves 6

2 large eggplants
2 to 3 red or green bell peppers (or a mixture of both)
1/2 cup extra-virgin olive oil
1 garlic clove, crushed through a press
Juice of 1/2 lemon
1/4 cup minced fresh parsley
Salt and freshly ground pepper

1. Pierce the eggplants in two or three places and char directly over a gas flame or under an electric broiler, turning them often until the skin is blackened. Cool. Peel and cut into cubes.
2. Without piercing, char the peppers as you did the eggplants. Cool, peel, core, and cut into strips.
3. In a serving bowl, combine the oil, garlic, lemon juice, parsley, and salt and pepper to taste. Add the peppers and toss. Using a slotted spoon, remove the peppers to another bowl. Add the eggplants to the dressing and toss well.
4. Return the peppers to the serving bowl, arranging them all around the eggplants in a decorative fashion. Garnish with additional fresh parsley, if desired, and serve.

$^1/_2$ cup olive oil
$^1/_4$ cup plus 1 tablespoon red wine vinegar
1 garlic clove, minced
2 to 3 fresh basil leaves, minced
Salt and freshly ground pepper
2 medium potatoes, boiled and diced
2 cups string beans, blanched and cut into bite-sized pieces
1 cup ripe olives, pitted
2 tablespoons capers, drained
1 small head romaine or Boston lettuce, torn into bite-sized pieces
3 hard-cooked eggs, sliced

INSALATA GENOVESE
Genoa-Style Salad
Serves 6

1. In a small bowl, combine the oil, vinegar, garlic, and basil and season with salt and pepper to taste. Whisk until well blended.
2. In a bowl, combine the potatoes, string beans, olives, and capers. Add the dressing and toss well.
3. Scatter the lettuce at bottom and sides of a serving bowl and pile the vegetables on top. Decorate with the sliced egg. Just before serving, toss well.

INSALATA ALLA SICILIANA
Sicilian-Style Salad
Serves 6

1 orange
1 garlic clove, crushed through a press
$1/4$ cup olive oil
1 tablespoon red wine vinegar (optional)
1 head curly chicory or escarole, tender parts only

1. Peel the orange and slice it into rounds. Cut the rounds into quarters. Make sure to collect the juice.
2. In a salad bowl, combine the orange juice and garlic. Pour in the oil and vinegar (if used), toss, and let stand until ready to serve.
3. Add the salad greens and toss before serving.

NOTE: This salad is also good when made with spinach.

INSALATA DI CAVOLI ALLA TORINESE
Turin-Style Cabbage Salad
Serves 6

$1/2$ head crisp white cabbage, coarsely shredded
$1/2$ head crisp red cabbage, coarsely shredded
$1/4$ teaspoon celery seed (optional)
$1/4$ cup olive oil
5 to 6 anchovy fillets, coarsely chopped

1. In a salad bowl, mound the white cabbage in the center with a ring of red cabbage around it. Sprinkle with the celery seed, if desired.
2. In a saucepan, combine the oil and anchovies over low heat and cook, mashing the anchovies until reduced to a paste, about 5 minutes. Pour the dressing over the salad, toss, and serve.

INSALATA CAPRICCIOSA
Capricious Salad
Serves 6 to 8

This salad has the colors of Christmas. Keep it in mind for your holidays. I often serve it as an antipasto on Christmas Eve.

3 ripe avocados
1 lemon
3 red bell peppers
$3/4$ pound fresh mushrooms
1 garlic clove

1/2 teaspoon Dijon-style mustard
1/4 cup olive oil
3 to 4 sprigs fresh parsley, minced

1. Peel, pit, and slice the avocados. Arrange the slices all around the edge of a serving dish. Sprinkle with a little lemon to prevent discoloration.
2. Roast the peppers over a gas flame or under the broiler. Peel away the charred skin, core, and cut the peppers into strips. Arrange the strips in a circle inside the avocado slices.
3. Quarter the mushrooms (or keep them whole if small) and place in a bowl. Squeeze the juice of half the lemon over the avocado slices and mushrooms. Toss the mushrooms and pile in the center of a serving dish.
4. In a small cup or bowl, mash the garlic and stir in the mustard. Add the oil and the remaining lemon juice. Beat with a fork and pour the dressing over the avocado slices, the peppers, and the mushrooms. Chill.
5. Just before serving, sprinkle with the parsley.

Calpurnia was Caesar's wife. I think she deserves a salad too.

INSALATA DI CALPURNIA
Calpurnia's Salad
Serves 6

1 bunch romaine lettuce
2 hard-cooked eggs, sliced in the round
1 can (2 ounces) rolled anchovy fillets with capers
1 cup cooked shellfish such as shrimp, lobster, or crab meat
1/4 cup olive oil
Juice of 1 lemon
Parsley sprigs

1. Tear the lettuce into bite-sized pieces and place in a salad bowl. Arrange the sliced eggs around the perimeter of the bowl and top the eggs with the rolled anchovies.
2. In a mixing bowl, combine the shellfish and oil, and season with lemon juice to taste. Toss well and place in the center of the salad bowl. Decorate with the parsley sprigs and toss just before serving.

INSALATA RUSSA
Russian Salad
Serves 6 to 8

Insalata Russa is eaten all over the Italian peninsula. A must at formal dinners and banquets, this classic dish got its exotic name from an Italian chef who invented it at the court of the Russian tsars.

1 pound seasonal vegetables—zucchini, string beans, peas, artichokes—trimmed, diced, and blanched
1 bunch broccoli or cauliflower, trimmed, cut into florets, and blanched
2 potatoes, boiled and diced
$1/4$ cup plus 2 tablespoons olive oil
$1/4$ cup red wine vinegar
1 small garlic clove, minced (optional)
1 sour pickle, chopped
Juice of 1 lemon
Salt and freshly ground pepper
2 cups mayonnaise, preferably homemade (see page 41)
1 small jar red pimientos, for garnish
1 jar Italian pickled artichokes, for garnish

1. Combine the seasonal vegetables, broccoli, and potatoes in a large bowl. Toss to distribute evenly.
2. In a mixing bowl, combine the oil, vinegar, garlic (if using), pickle, lemon juice, and salt and pepper to taste. Mix well and pour over the vegetables. Toss well to coat.
3. Add 1 cup of the mayonnaise and toss. Adjust the seasoning if necessary. Spoon the salad into a flat serving dish. Spread evenly and cover with the remaining 1 cup mayonnaise. Decorate with the pimientos and artichokes before serving.

NOTE: Shellfish can be added if you wish. Leftover Russian Salad is excellent as a stuffing for such vegetables as tomatoes, cooked artichokes, or avocados.

8 leaves romaine lettuce
1 small head radicchio
2 heads Belgian endive or escarole, white parts only
1 teaspoon grainy mustard
¼ cup virgin olive oil
3 tablespoons red wine vinegar

INSALATA COLORATA
Colorful Salad
Serves 6

1. Tear the lettuce and radicchio into bite-sized pieces and cut the endive into ¼-inch lengths.
2. In a salad bowl, whisk together the mustard, oil, and vinegar. Add the salad, toss, and serve immediately.

Fulvio Tramontina, the friendly owner of the Salta in Bocca restaurant in New York, is as patriotic as I am when it comes to the flag of our country. We even put its colors in our foods.

INSALATA TRICOLORE
Tricolored Salad
Serves 4

12 ounces fresh mozzarella cheese (preferably made from buffalo's milk), sliced
2 heads radicchio
2 bunches arugula
3 tomatoes, sliced (about 1 pound)
2 heads Belgian endive
A few basil leaves

DRESSING

4 tablespoons virgin olive oil
1 tablespoon *aceto balsamico* (balsamic vinegar) or red wine vinegar
Salt and freshly ground pepper

1. Divide the mozzarella among four salad plates and place it in the center. Arrange leaves of the radicchio, arugula, and endive and the tomato slices around the cheese.
2. In a small bowl, mix the oil, vinegar, and salt and pepper to taste. Drizzle the dressing over the salad just before serving. Decorate each dish with basil leaves.

GIARDINIERA
Garden Greens
Serves 8

This dish can be served as an antipasto or a salad.

16 asparagus spears, trimmed (see NOTE)
$^{1}/_{2}$ pound string beans, trimmed
1 small head cauliflower, cored and cut into florets
1 small head broccoli, trimmed and left in long stems
2 hard-cooked eggs, quartered

DRESSING

$^{1}/_{2}$ cup mayonnaise (see page 41)
2 tablespoons lemon juice
1 tablespoon yogurt
A touch of garlic, mashed through a garlic press
1 tablespoon minced fresh parsley

1. In a large pot of boiling water, blanch the vegetables one at a time, keeping them very crisp.
2. Arrange vegetables on a serving dish and decorate with egg quarters.
3. Combine all the ingredients of the dressing, place in a small bowl, and set in the middle of the vegetable dish.

NOTE: Use zucchini cut lengthwise when asparagus is not in season. Sunchokes or Jerusalem artichokes are very good in this dish, as are red beets.

INSALATA DI TONNO MAMMA E PAPÀ
Mother and Father's Tuna Salad
Serves 6

This was my parents' favorite salad—perfect for supper after a big midday Sunday dinner.

2 cans (7 ounces each) Italian oil-packed tunafish
1 medium red onion, peeled and thinly sliced
1 lemon, cut into 6 wedges
Crusty Italian bread

1. Drain the tuna, reserving the oil. Arrange the tuna on a serving dish and flake it with a fork. Scatter the onion rings over the tuna and drizzle with the reserved oil.
2. Serve with lemon wedges and a loaf of crusty bread.

6 red or green bell peppers, or a mixture of both
1 garlic clove, minced
2 to 3 tablespoons olive oil
Minced fresh parsley

PEPERONI ARROSTITI
Roasted Peppers
Serves 6

1. Roast the peppers by placing them directly on the flame of the gas burner or directly under a broiler. Turn often, until the skin is completely charred. Drop the peppers into a brown bag and seal the top to let them steam. (This will facilitate peeling.)
2. Peel, core, seed, and cut the peppers into strips.
3. In a serving dish, combine the garlic and oil. Add the peppers and toss. Sprinkle with the parsley and serve.

6 *freselle* (twice-baked bread slices)
1 garlic clove
1 hot chili pepper (optional)
Virgin olive oil
Salt
6 to 8 very ripe tomatoes, halved
Fresh basil or oregano leaves

PANZANELLA DELLA CASA
Bread Salad
Serves 8

1. Sprinkle the bread with a little water, if desired, and rub with garlic and hot pepper (if using). Brush each slice with olive oil, sprinkle with salt, and squash the halved tomatoes on the bread.
2. Decorate with basil leaves or oregano and serve.

NOTE: Add a sprinkling of vinegar, if desired. *Freselle* are available in Italian or specialty food shops.

INSALATINA INVERNALE
Little Winter Salad
Serves 6

1 garlic clove, mashed through a press
¼ cup olive oil
About 1 tablespoon lemon juice
2 green bell peppers, roasted, peeled, and cut into strips
3 beets, boiled, peeled, and sliced or diced
1 small bunch arugula or fresh spinach

1. In a salad bowl, combine the garlic, oil, and lemon juice. Add the pepper strips and toss; set aside.
2. Just before serving, add the beets and arugula and toss well to coat the vegetables.

NOTE: For roasting peppers, see page 33.

INSALATA ALLA NEVE
Snowy Salad
Serves 6

1 head romaine, Bibb, or Boston lettuce
1 ripe avocado
¼ cup olive oil
½ teaspoon grainy mustard
1 small garlic clove, minced
2 tablespoons red wine vinegar
2 tablespoons fresh lemon juice
2 hard-cooked eggs

1. Wash and dry the lettuce. Tear it into bite-sized pieces.
2. Peel and pit the avocado. In a salad bowl, mash the avocado pulp and add the oil, mustard, garlic, vinegar, and lemon juice.
3. Separate the cooked egg whites from the yolks and chop each. Add the yolks to the avocado mixture and mix to blend. Add the lettuce and set aside.
4. Sprinkle the white of the eggs on top of the salad. Toss before serving.

DRESSING

3/4 cup olive oil
1/2 cup red wine vinegar
1 teaspoon Dijon-style mustard
1 teaspoon tomato paste
2 tablespoons capers
1 sour pickle
1 garlic clove
1 bunch fresh parsley
Pinch of tarragon
1/4 cup mayonnaise (see page 41)

SALAD

1 large head cauliflower
1 head radicchio or copper lettuce
1 head green-leaf or romaine lettuce
4 to 5 radishes, sliced
4 plum tomatoes, thinly sliced
1 can (8 ounces) black olives
Freshly ground pepper

INSALATA DELLA VIGILIA DI CAPODANNO
New Year's Eve Salad
Serves 6

1. In a food processor, combine all of the ingredients for the dressing. Process until liquid and set aside in the processor.
2. Core the cauliflower. Peel and cut the stems and core into small pieces. Divide the cauliflower into small florets. Place in a salad bowl. Whirl the dressing to mix it and pour over the cauliflower. Cover and refrigerate.
3. Tear the lettuce leaves into bite-sized pieces, reserving the curly tops, and add to the bowl around the cauliflower. Mound the radish slices in the center of the cauliflower mixture. Place the reserved lettuce leaves around the sides of the bowl and encircle the radishes with the tomato slices. Decorate with the olives and grind a few twists of fresh pepper on top.
4. Just before serving, toss all of the ingredients together.

INSALATA CROCCANTE
Crunchy Salad
Serves 6 to 8

1 fennel bulb, thinly sliced
1 carrot, cut into thin rounds or julienne
2 to 3 Jerusalem artichokes (sunchokes), cut into wedges
1 tablespoon capers, drained
Fresh lemon juice
1 can (7 ounces) Italian oil-packed tunafish
Parsley sprigs

1. In a large bowl, combine the fennel, carrot, Jerusalem artichokes, capers, and lemon juice to taste. Pour the oil from the tuna over the salad and flake the tuna. Add it and toss the salad, distributing the ingredients evenly.
2. Sprinkle the salad with additional fresh lemon juice to taste and garnish with the parsley.

NOTE: If you use water-packed tuna, add about 2 tablespoons of olive oil to dress the salad.

INSALATA VARIEGATA
Streaked Salad
Serves 6 to 8

1 small head radicchio or copper lettuce
1 head Boston lettuce
1 cucumber, peeled
2 red beets, cooked and peeled
1 small garlic clove, crushed through a press
¼ cup olive oil
2 tablespoons red wine vinegar
Freshly ground pepper
½ teaspoon Dijon-style mustard (optional)
A few leaves of tarragon, dill, or parsley

1. Wash the salad leaves and wrap them in paper towels. Thinly slice the cucumber and set aside. Slice the beets and set aside.
2. In a salad bowl, combine the garlic, oil, vinegar, pepper, mustard (if using), and the snipped herbs. Beat the mixture with a fork.
3. Break the lettuces into bite-sized pieces and add to the bowl. Arrange the cucumbers and beets all around the bowl. Toss at the last minute. The juices of the beets will "variegate" or streak the salad.

NOTE: Untossed salads can be kept for several hours in the refrigerator covered with a few sheets of dampened paper towel.

This is my daily salad and my usual dressing. Any fresh, seasonal ingredients can be added to this salad—tomatoes, onions, radishes, cucumbers. I do not add salt since the dressing is flavorful and the touch of mustard gives all of the saltiness that's needed.

INSALATA GIORNALIERA
Everyday Salad
Serves 6

Any kind of lettuce
Fresh vegetables

DRESSING

1 small garlic clove, crushed through a press
1 teaspoon grainy mustard
About 2¹/₂ teaspoons red wine vinegar
3 tablespoons olive oil
Freshly ground pepper

1. Wash the lettuce and dry it. Tear it into bite-sized pieces. Chop or cut the other vegetables.

2. In a small bowl, combine the dressing ingredients and mix vigorously with a fork. Just before serving, pour the dressing over the salad and toss.

NOTE: The dressing for almost any salad can be prepared in the serving bowl. Just place your tossing fork and spoon in the bowl, put the greens over them, and refrigerate, covered with a few sheets of dampened paper towel. It will keep crisp for hours. Toss just before serving.

Desserts

4 eggs, separated
1½ cups granulated sugar
1 envelope unflavored gelatin
1 teaspoon cornstarch
Juice of 3 lemons (about ¾ cup)
4 tablespoons orange-flavored liqueur
1½ cups heavy cream
3 tablespoons confectioners' sugar

SPUMA DI LIMONE
Lemon Mousse
Serves 6 to 8

1. In a mixing bowl, beat the egg yolks until lemon-colored. Gradually add the granulated sugar and continue beating until quite thick.
2. Bring ¼ cup of water to a boil. Remove from heat, add the gelatin, and stir until completely dissolved.
3. In a mixing bowl, combine the cornstarch with a few tablespoons of the lemon juice. Stir in the gelatin and add to the egg mixture. Place in a double boiler over simmering water and cook, stirring, until the mixture thickens. Remove from the heat

and add 2 tablespoons of the orange liqueur. Pour into a bowl and chill.

4. In a bowl, whip the cream with the remaining 2 tablespoons orange liqueur and the confectioners' sugar. This can be done in the bowl of a food processor fitted with a plastic blade.

5. In another bowl, beat the egg whites until stiff. Stir a few spoonfuls of the egg whites and the whipped cream into the gelatin mixture to lighten it. Fold in the remaining egg whites and whipped cream. Pour the mousse into a serving bowl or individual bowls and chill for 1 to 2 hours before serving.

SEMIFREDDO DI RICOTTA ED AMARETTI
Ricotta and Amaretti Mousse
Serves 6 to 8

Ricotta is a light cheese which lends itself to many variations. It is more flavorful and creamier than cottage cheese, mixes well with sweet and savory foods, is ideal for stuffing, and is deliciously refreshing by itself.

2 tablespoons mixed candied fruit
3 tablespoons raisins
2 tablespoons chopped walnuts
1/4 cup plus 2 tablespoons rum
1 1/2 pounds fresh whole-milk ricotta cheese
3/4 cup sugar
1/4 teaspoon vanilla extract
2 squares (2 ounces) semisweet chocolate, chopped or grated
4 *amaretti* cookies, crumbled

1. Combine the candied fruits, raisins, and walnuts in a bowl and pour on the rum. Set aside.

2. In a food processor or blender, whip the ricotta. Add the sugar and vanilla. Add the chocolate and the rum mixture and process, turning the machine on and off, to mix the ingredients well.

3. Pour the mixture into a serving bowl or into individual stemmed glasses. Top with the crumbled *amaretti* and chill for at least 1 hour.

2 pints strawberries
3 tablespoons strawberry-flavored liqueur
1½ cups hot milk
1 envelope unflavored gelatin
3 egg yolks
3 tablespoons granulated sugar
½ teaspoon vanilla extract
1 cup heavy cream
1½ teaspoons confectioners' sugar
About 24 ladyfingers
2 tablespoons orange-flavored liqueur

SEMIFREDDO DI FRAGOLE
Strawberry Mousse
Serves 6 to 8

1. Stem the strawberries and halve them. Place the berries in a bowl and sprinkle with the strawberry liqueur. In a colander set over a shallow bowl, drain the berries, reserving the liquid.

2. In a medium saucepan, combine the milk, gelatin, and any liquid that was drained from the fruit. Warm over moderate heat to dissolve the gelatin.

3. In a zabaglione pot or in a double boiler, combine the egg yolks with the granulated sugar and beat with an electric mixer for 5 minutes. One tablespoon at a time, add the hot milk mixture and continue beating. Place the pot over very low heat and cook, stirring and beating, until the custard comes to a boil. Remove from the heat, stir in the vanilla, and place the pot in a bowl of ice. Continue beating until the custard is cold.

4. In a bowl, whip the cream with the confectioners' sugar and fold into the chilled custard. Line a 1½-quart soufflé dish or charlotte mold with a large sheet of plastic wrap, making sure that extra wrap hangs over the sides. Line the bottom and sides of the prepared dish with ladyfingers, cutting them to fit if necessary. Sprinkle the ladyfingers with the orange liqueur.

5. Pour some of the custard into the prepared dish and top with a layer of strawberries. Continue layering until all of the fruit and custard is used. Top the dish with a layer of ladyfingers. (If you wish, you can also use more ladyfingers and layer throughout.) Freeze for at least 2 hours, until firm.

6. When the mousse is firm, unmold it, remove the plastic wrap, and slice into serving portions.

SPUMA DI PESCHE AL RUM
Cold Peach Soufflé with Rum
Serves 8

4 to 5 large peaches
$1/2$ cup honey
$1/2$ teaspoon almond extract
3 tablespoons rum
$1/4$ cup fresh orange juice
2 tablespoons fresh lemon juice
$1^1/2$ tablespoons unflavored gelatin
1 cup heavy cream
$1/2$ teaspoon vanilla extract
4 egg whites
Pinch of salt

1. Tie a parchment or foil collar around a $1^1/2$-quart soufflé dish, or individual ramekins. Blanch the peaches in boiling water for a few seconds. Peel and quarter the fruit; discard the pits.
2. In a food processor or blender, purée the peaches with the honey and the almond extract.
3. In a small saucepan, cook the rum, orange juice, and lemon juice over low heat until hot. Remove from the heat and add the gelatin, stirring until dissolved. Blend the gelatin mixture into the peach purée and turn into a large bowl.
4. In a mixing bowl, whip the cream and vanilla until stiff. Gently fold the cream into the peach mixture.
5. In another bowl, beat the egg whites with the salt until stiff. Gently fold into the peach mixture and spoon into the prepared soufflé dish. Chill for about 3 hours.

ZUPPA INGLESE CASA MIA
Home-Style Zuppa Inglese
Serves 8 to 10

1 batch Pan di Spagna Luciana Amore (sponge cake, see page 187)
2 cups Crema di Mamma (custard, page 188)
$1^1/2$ tablespoons unsweetened cocoa powder
3 to 4 tablespoons rum
3 to 4 tablespoons flavored liqueur, such as Grand Marnier or Cointreau
2 tablespoons confectioners' sugar
1 teaspoon cinnamon

1. A day or two in advance, make the sponge cake according to the recipe.

2. Divide the *crema* into two parts. Mix one half with the cocoa.

3. Cut the sponge cake into thin slices and place one layer in the bottom of a crystal bowl. Sprinkle generously with rum. Spoon some of the "white" *crema* on the cake and smooth with a spatula. Cover with a second layer of cake slices. Sprinkle with the liqueur and spoon on some of the "chocolate" *crema*; smooth the top.

4. Continue layering, alternating white crema with chocolate and the rum with the liqueur, finishing with a layer of the sponge slices. Chill for at least 2 hours or overnight.

5. In a small bowl, combine the confectioners' sugar and cinnamon. Sprinkle over the top of the cake just before serving.

NOTE: This cake is better if prepared one day in advance. Keep chilled until 30 minutes before serving.

PAN DI SPAGNA LUCIANA AMORE
Luciana Amore's Sponge Cake
Serves 6 to 8

4 eggs, separated
1/4 teaspoon lemon or vanilla extract
3/4 cup sugar
3/4 cup plus 1 tablespoon all-purpose flour
1 teaspoon baking powder

1. Preheat the oven to 350°. Lightly butter and flour a 9 × 5 × 3-inch standard loaf pan. Set aside.

2. In a bowl, beat the egg yolks, extract, and sugar until fluffy and lemon-colored. Sift in the flour and baking powder and mix well. The batter will be a little stiff.

3. In another bowl, beat the egg whites until stiff. Gently but quickly, fold the egg whites into the egg-yolk mixture. Pour into the prepared pan. Bake for 45 minutes without opening the oven door.

4. Remove the cake and "hang" it, still in the pan, upside down, on the corners of 4 cans. Let cool.

5. Slide a thin spatula or knife all around the cake to help remove it more easily from the pan.

CREMA DI MAMMA
Mama's Custard
Makes 2 cups

The best pot in which to make this *crema* is a zabaglione pot. In any case, a copper or enameled pot should be used.

4 egg yolks
3/4 cup sugar
3 tablespoons flour
2 cups milk
1 or 2 strips lemon peel
1 teaspoon vanilla extract

1. In the pot, combine the yolks, sugar, and flour. Mix with a wire whisk until smooth.
2. Slowly add the milk, stirring until mixture liquefies. Add the lemon peel.
3. Place pot over medium-low heat and cook the custard, stirring constantly, until it starts to "puff." Let it puff 2 or 3 times, but be careful not to let it come to a full boil.
4. Remove from heat and add the vanilla. Stir and turn into a china bowl.

NOTE: My mother always used a vanilla bean, which she added together with the lemon peel. Afterward she would remove the bean, rinse it, let it dry, and store it in a jar. It was reused many times.

ZABAGLIONE CLASSICO
Classic Zabaglione
Serves 6

6 egg yolks
1/2 cup sugar
1/4 cup Marsala wine

1. In a zabaglione pot, or a double boiler, combine the egg yolks, sugar, and Marsala. Cook over boiling water, beating constantly, until the mixture thickens and mounds like whipped cream.
2. Serve alone or as a sauce for fruit or sponge cakes.

12 ounces semisweet chocolate morsels
5 eggs, separated
3 tablespoons orange-flavored liqueur
1 teaspoon ground espresso coffee
1½ cups heavy cream
Pinch of cream of tartar

BUDINO DI CIOCCOLATA
Chocolate Pudding
Serves 8

1. In a double boiler, melt the chocolate over hot, but not boiling, water. Off the heat, cool the chocolate, stirring, and add the egg yolks one at a time, beating after each addition.
2. In a small saucepan, bring the liqueur to a boil. Stir in the coffee and remove from the heat. Set aside to cool.
3. Strain the coffee-liqueur mixture and add to the cooled chocolate.
4. In a bowl, whip the cream until stiff. Refrigerate
5. In another bowl, beat the egg whites until foamy. Add the cream of tartar and continue beating until stiff. Gently and thoroughly, fold the egg whites into the chocolate mixture, a little at a time. Fold in the whipped cream in the same manner. Pour the *budino* into individual glasses or a glass bowl and chill for about 3 hours before serving.

NOTE: This pudding is nice when served with a dollop of whipped cream topped by a roasted coffee bean. It can be stored overnight in the refrigerator, but it is better when eaten the day it is made.

4 egg yolks
¼ cup sugar
2 tablespoons Aurum or other orange-flavored liqueur
¾ cup heavy cream, whipped

SPUMONE ALL'AURUM
Golden Froth
Serves 6

1. In a zabaglione pot or in the top of a double boiler, combine the egg yolks, sugar, and Aurum with 3 tablespoons water. Mix well and cook over very low heat (or simmering water), beating until the mixture feels warm to the touch. Continue beating until fluffy and light; chill.
2. Gently fold the whipped cream into the chilled egg mixture. Turn the mixture into a bowl or stemmed glasses and cover with plastic wrap. Freeze until firm, about 2 hours.

BUDINO DI RICOTTA
Ricotta Pudding
Serves 8

¹/₂ cup fine dry bread crumbs
¹/₄ cup raisins
¹/₄ cup mixed candied fruits, diced
¹/₄ cup rum
4 eggs
1¹/₂ pounds whole-milk ricotta cheese
¹/₄ cup all-purpose flour
¹/₄ cup plus 1 tablespoon sugar
Pinch of cinnamon
1 teaspoon freshly grated lemon zest
¹/₂ teaspoon vanilla extract
Butter for soufflé dish
Sugar and cinnamon, mixed together

1. Preheat the oven to 350°. Butter a standard 1¹/₂-quart soufflé dish and coat with bread crumbs, shaking out the excess.
2. In a small bowl, combine the raisins and candied fruit. Pour the rum over and let stand.
3. Separate 3 of the eggs. In a mixing bowl, combine 1 whole egg with the egg yolks and beat until frothy. Slowly add the ricotta and beat again.
4. On a sheet of wax paper, combine the flour, sugar, and cinnamon. Add to the ricotta mixture along with the lemon zest and the vanilla. Mix well and add the candied fruit–rum mixture.
5. In a bowl, beat the egg whites until stiff. Gently fold the whites into the ricotta mixture. Pour into the prepared soufflé dish and bake until the top is nicely colored, about 1 hour.
6. Let the pudding cool in the oven before unmolding onto a serving dish. Dust with a mixture of sugar and cinnamon before serving.

NOTE: This pudding will fall when cool.

DOUGH

2²/₃ cups all-purpose flour
¹/₂ cup sugar
12 tablespoons (1¹/₂ sticks) unsalted butter
2 egg yolks
2 tablespoons Marsala wine
¹/₂ teaspoon baking powder

FILLING

1¹/₂ cups toasted almonds
³/₄ cup sugar
Pinch of cinnamon
1 teaspoon lemon extract
Orange marmalade
1¹/₂ cups Crema di Mamma (custard, see page 188)
6 egg whites
Confectioners' sugar, for decoration

CROSTATA DI CREMA JOLANDA
Jolanda's Cream Pie
Serves 6 to 8

1. Make the dough: In a mixing bowl, combine the flour and sugar. Add the butter and quickly work with the fingers until the mixture resembles coarse meal.
2. Add the egg yolks, Marsala, and baking powder, using additional Marsala if the mixture is too crumbly. Turn onto a floured board and form the dough into a ball; do not handle too much. Wrap in plastic or foil and chill for about 1 hour.
3. Make the filling: In a food processor, combine the almonds and sugar and chop until fine. Turn the mixture into a mixing bowl and add the cinnamon and lemon extract. Set aside.
4. Preheat the oven to 375°. Butter a 10-inch pie pan. On a lightly floured surface, roll out the dough ¹/₂ inch thick. Line the prepared pan and trim. Brush the pastry with the marmalade and fill the shell with the custard.
5. Lightly beat the egg whites and combine with the almond mixture. Pour over the custard and smooth the top. Bake for 30 minutes, or until the top is set and the crust is lightly browned.
6. Cool completely on a rack. Just before serving, dust with confectioners' sugar.

CROSTATA DI PESCHE CON RICOTTA
Peach and Ricotta Pie
Serves 10

DOUGH

2¹/₂ cups all-purpose flour
¹/₂ cup granulated sugar
1 cup very finely chopped walnuts
Grated zest of 1 lemon
8 tablespoons (1 stick) butter, chilled and cut into bits
4 egg yolks
1 tablespoon rum or Cognac
3 to 4 tablespoons ice water, if necessary

FILLING

5 medium peaches
Juice of ¹/₂ lemon
4 tablespoons confectioners' sugar
³/₄ cup whole-milk ricotta cheese
1 cup heavy cream
¹/₄ teaspoon almond extract
¹/₄ teaspoon vanilla extract
²/₃ cup apricot jam
2 tablespoons apricot or peach liqueur

1. Make the dough: In a mixing bowl or food processor, combine the flour, sugar, nuts, lemon zest, and butter. Work the butter into the flour until the mixture resembles coarse meal.
2. In a bowl, lightly beat the egg yolks with the rum or Cognac. Add to the flour mixture, stirring with a fork. Gather the dough into a ball; if too crumbly, add a bit of the ice water. Wrap the dough and chill for 30 minutes or longer.
3. Prepare the filling: In a pot of boiling water, poach the peaches until the skins come off easily. Cool, halve, pit, and peel the peaches. Set aside one whole half of a peach and slice the remaining halves evenly. Sprinkle the slices with the lemon juice and 1 tablespoon of the confectioners' sugar. Toss.
4. Preheat the oven to 425°. Butter a 10-inch quiche or pie pan. Roll out the dough and line the bottom and sides of the prepared pan. Pierce the bottom crust with a fork, line with foil, and fill with aluminum pie weights or beans. Bake for 15 minutes. Remove the weights and foil and bake for a few minutes longer, just to dry the bottom.
5. With a food processor or electric mixer, combine the ricotta

and remaining 3 tablespoons sugar. Process for a few seconds. Start adding the cream, a little at a time, and whip. Add the almond and vanilla extracts. Pour the mixture into the baked crust and smooth the top. Place the reserved peach half in the center of the tart and arrange the slices all around.

6. In a saucepan, combine the apricot jam and liqueur over low heat. When melted, strain, and drizzle the mixture over the peaches.

7. Chill for about 3 hours, but serve at more-or-less room temperature.

CROSTATA DI MELE AL CROCCANTE
Apple Tart with Croccante
Serves 8

Butter for pan

5 crisp apples, such as Cortland, Baldwin, Northern Spy, or Golden Delicious

1 batch *crostata* (tart) dough (see page 194)

4 ounces Italian *croccante* (see NOTE), chopped, or use blanched, peeled, toasted almonds

2 tablespoons sugar

1½ teaspoons unsalted butter

3 to 4 tablespoons apple jelly

1 tablespoon kirschwasser

1. Preheat the oven to 400°. Butter a 10-inch tart or quiche pan. Peel, core, and thinly slice the apples; set aside.

2. Roll out the dough and fit it into the bottom and sides of the prepared pan. Pierce the bottom with a fork and sprinkle with the *croccante* or almonds.

3. Arrange the apple slices in overlapping concentric rings. Sprinkle with the sugar and dot with the butter. Bake for 45 to 50 minutes, until the crust is golden brown. Set on a rack to cool.

4. In a small saucepan, combine the apple jelly with the kirschwasser. Melt over low heat and paint the tart. Cool before slicing.

NOTE: *Croccante* is a nougat similar to peanut or almond brittle.

PASTA PER CROSTATA
Tart Dough
Makes 1 piecrust

8 tablespoons (1 stick) unsalted butter, chilled
$^1/_2$ cup sugar
2 cups all-purpose flour
2 eggs
1 tablespoon flavored liqueur

1. In a mixing bowl, cut the butter into 7 or 8 pieces. Add the sugar and flour and work with the fingers or a pastry blender until the mixture resembles coarse meal. Add the eggs and liqueur and mix with a fork. Gather the dough into a ball. If too crumbly, add a few drops of ice water; do not handle the dough too much.
2. Wrap in plastic or foil and chill for at least 30 minutes before rolling out.

NOTE: This dough can be made in a food processor. It freezes quite well and can be made well in advance.

Tips for my pie pastry:
• Use vegetable shortening for flakier pastry.
• Use butter for crumbly pastry.
• Use lard for sturdy and flaky pastry.
• Use shortening and butter in equal parts to make a crust that is similar to lard pastry.

TORTA DI AMARETTI
Amaretti Torte
Serves 10

10 *amaretti* (Italian macaroons)
4 ounces semisweet chocolate
$^1/_2$ pound (2 sticks) unsalted butter, at room temperature
1 cup granulated sugar
5 eggs, separated
$^1/_2$ cup all-purpose flour
1 tablespoon Aurum or orange-flavored liqueur
Confectioners' sugar, for decoration
5 or 6 *amarettini*, for decoration (optional)

1. Preheat the oven to 350°. Butter a 10-inch cake pan. In a blender or food processor, pulverize the *amaretti* and chocolate.
2. In a bowl, cream together the butter and sugar until fluffy. Add the egg yolks, one at a time, and beat for 10 minutes.

3. Gradually add the flour and the *amaretti*-chocolate mixture, beating well after each addition. Add the Aurum or liqueur.

4. In another bowl, beat the egg whites until stiff. Fold the whites into the *amaretti* mixture and pour into the prepared pan. Bake for 45 minutes, until golden. Cool and unmold cake.

5. Before serving, sprinkle the torte with confectioners' sugar. Decorate with a few *amarettini* around the edges and the middle.

NOTE: A bit of orange marmalade under the *amarettini* will make them stick to the cake. This cake is better the next day. Keep in mind that the cake doesn't rise much.

---

5 egg yolks
¼ cup cornstarch or potato starch
½ cup sugar
1 tablespoon unflavored gelatin
2 cups light cream, warmed
½ cup strong freshly brewed espresso coffee
2 tablespoons coffee-flavored liqueur, such as Tia Maria or Kahlua
1 cup heavy cream, whipped

CREMOLATA AL CAFFÈ
Coffee Pudding
Serves 6

1. In a copper zabaglione pot or a nonreactive saucepan, whisk the egg yolks with the cornstarch. Add the sugar and gelatin and whisk well.

2. Pour in the light cream, a little at a time, stirring constantly, until the mixture looks liquid and smooth. Add the espresso.

3. Place the pan over very low heat and cook, stirring constantly, until the custard thickens. Remove from the heat and cool for 15 minutes.

4. Add the liqueur and stir to blend. Fold in half of the whipped cream. Spoon the pudding into stemmed glasses and decorate with the remaining whipped cream. Chill.

NOTE: Leftover egg whites freeze quite well in ice-cube trays. When hard, remove and bag them and keep in freezer.

BOCCONOTTI ALL' ABRUZZESE
Little Stuffed Pies
Makes 10 to 12 *bocconotti*

These Abruzzese pastries are traditionally served throughout the Christmas holidays.

DOUGH

2 cups all-purpose flour
$1/2$ cup sugar
8 tablespoons (1 stick) unsalted butter
2 whole eggs
2 egg yolks

FILLING

1 cup toasted almonds
6 tablespoons sugar
6 tablespoons unsweetened cocoa powder
Grated zest of 1 lemon
Pinch of cinnamon
Sweet wine such as sherry, Marsala, or Vin Santo

1. Make the dough: In a food processor, combine $1 1/2$ cups of the flour with the sugar. Add the butter and process until the mixture resembles coarse meal. Add the eggs and egg yolks and process until a ball of dough forms on the blade, adding more flour when and if necessary. The dough should be consistent. Wrap in plastic and chill.

2. Make the filling: In a food processor, combine the almonds with the sugar and process until fine. Add the cocoa, lemon zest, cinnamon, and just enough wine to make the mixture creamy but not too wet.

3. Generously butter the *bocconotti* forms (or use brioche molds or a muffin tin) and set aside. Roll out half of the dough $1/8$ inch thick. Cut the dough into 5-inch rounds. Place each piece of dough in a form, and press lightly so that it adheres to the sides. The dough will overhang a bit; trim it evenly. Spoon some of the filling into each form, but do not overfill.

4. Preheat the oven to 375°. Roll out the remaining dough $1/8$ inch thick. Cut into 4-inch rounds and cover each pastry, pressing the dough into place over the filling. Seal all the way around by pushing the dough together, allowing any overhanging dough to fall away.

5. Place the *bocconotti* on a cookie sheet and bake for 20 to 25 minutes, until lightly browned. Cool, unmold, and dust with a mixture of sugar and cinnamon if desired. Store airtight in tins.

I like to serve this sherbet at Thanksgiving, probably because I am not very fond of cranberry sauce! The recipe is an adaptation of one of food writer Bert Greene's delicious desserts.

SORBETTO DI MORTELLE E ANANAS
Cranberry and Pineapple Sherbet
Serves 6 to 8

1¼ cups sugar
1 pound fresh cranberries
2 cups fresh pineapple, chopped
1 orange, peeled, seeded, and chopped
1 tablespoon candied orange zest in syrup, or finely slivered orange zest
1 tablespoon kirschwasser, Aurum, Grand Marnier, or other liqueur
¼ teaspoon vanilla extract
Candied orange zest, for garnish

1. Place the sugar in a food processor and turn the machine on and off a few times to grind it very fine. Add the cranberries, pineapple, orange, and candied orange zest and process with on-and-off turns until finely chopped. Transfer to a mixing bowl and add the liqueur and vanilla. Cover and freeze until the mixture starts to freeze around the edges, about 2 hours.
2. Remove the *sorbetto* from the freezer. Scrape up the frozen parts and beat with an electric mixer, until well blended. Repeat the freezing/beating process twice and freeze overnight.
3. Spoon into serving dishes and garnish with strips of candied orange.

SORBETTO ALLO SPUMANTE
Champagne Sherbet
Serves 12

An ideal intermezzo or finale for the New Year's celebration.

> $1/2$ cup sugar
> 1 bottle (25.4 ounces) Italian spumante or other sparkling wine
> 2 tablespoons kirschwasser
> 2 cups cut-up fruit such as strawberries, lemons, oranges, or peaches
> Berries, for garnish (optional)

1. In a mixing bowl, combine the sugar, wine, and liqueur. Mix gently; do not break the bubbles in the spumante.
2. In a blender, purée the cut-up fruit and add to the wine mixture. Taste for sweetness and, if necessary, add a little more sugar.
3. Turn the mixture into 1 or 2 empty ice-cube trays and freeze for 3 hours, or overnight. Serve in individual glasses and garnish with berries.

VARIATION

During the holiday season, I add cranberries to the fruit to make it more traditional. Use only 1 cup of the other fruit and add this mixture:

> $1/2$ cup sugar
> $1/4$ cup water
> 1 cup cranberries, picked over and washed
> 1 tablespoon Aurum or other orange-flavored liqueur

1. In a saucepan, combine the sugar and water over low heat. Cook until the sugar dissolves. Increase the heat and boil for 5 minutes. Add the cranberries and cook, stirring often, until the liquid evaporates and mixture is sticky. Remove from the heat, add the liqueur, and cool.
2. Add the mixture to the other fruit and proceed as above with steps 2 and 3.

2 cups sliced ripe apricots, unpeeled
3 tablespoons confectioners' sugar
¼ cup plus 1 tablespoon Vov (zabaglione-flavored) liqueur
2 tablespoons frozen concentrated orange juice

SORBETTO DI ALBICOCCHE AL VOV
Apricot Sherbet with Vov
Serves 4 to 6

1. In a food processor or blender, process the apricots and sugar until they become an even purée. Add the Vov and the orange juice, and blend well.
2. Turn the mixture into a serving bowl or pour into individual glasses or bowls. Freeze for at least 3 hours, or overnight.
3. Remove from the freezer 30 minutes before serving.

NOTE: Vov is a zabaglione liqueur. You can also use it as a sauce. Decorate the *sorbetto* with strawberries or blueberries.

4 cups freshly brewed strong espresso coffee
Sugar to taste
2 tablespoons Amaretto or Sambuca Romana liqueur
1 cup heavy cream

GRANITA DI CAFFÈ
Coffee Ice
Serves 6 to 8

1. In a mixing bowl, combine the coffee, sugar, and liqueur. Stir well, let cool, and place in freezer for about 2 hours.
2. As soon as ice crystals start to form around the edges of the bowl, remove from the freezer and whip with an electric beater. Freeze again and repeat, whipping twice, every 2 hours. Freeze overnight.
3. When ready to serve, whip the heavy cream in a bowl. Remove the coffee *granita* from the freezer and spoon into stemmed glasses. Top each serving with a spoonful of whipped cream and serve immediately.

IL TARTUFO DI CARMELINA
Carmelina's Ice Cream Truffle
Serves 6

This is a family recipe, devised by my talented sister-in-law Carmelina Vita-Colonna.

1 pint dark chocolate ice cream
¹/₂ pound semisweet chocolate, coarsely chopped
2 tablespoons shortening
Centerba or Chartreuse liqueur

1. Let the ice cream soften just enough to be shaped into 6 balls. Set the balls on a foil-lined tray and freeze.
2. In the top of a double boiler set over hot water, melt the chocolate with a tablespoon of the shortening. Stir until melted. Remove from the heat and stir until cooled.
3. Remove the ice cream balls from the freezer. Quickly spoon some of the melted chocolate over each ball to coat the top and sides. Return to the freezer for 15 minutes, until the chocolate solidifies.
4. Add the remaining 1 tablespoon shortening to the remaining melted chocolate and place over hot water. Remove the ice cream balls from the freezer and turn them upside down. Spoon melted chocolate over so that each one is completely coated; freeze again.
5. Just before serving, place each *tartufo* on a serving dish or in an individual bowl. (Do not use fine crystal or china.) Set the bowls on a serving tray. Pour 3 to 4 tablespoons of liqueur over each *tartufo* and ignite. Serve while flaming; eat while the chocolate melts.

1 pint vanilla or coffee ice cream, softened
¹/₂ cup plus 1 tablespoon Sambuca Romana or anisette
¹/₂ cup plus 1 tablespoon coffee liqueur

SAMOCA AFFOGATO
Drowned Samoca
Serves 6

Divide the ice cream among 6 individual serving glasses. Combine the liqueurs and pour 3 tablespoons over each serving of ice cream. Serve at once.

NOTE: This dessert looks pretty decorated with coffee beans or chocolate curls.

1 cup all-purpose flour
1 cup chopped raisins or 1¹/₂ cups chopped mixed raisins and candied fruits
¹/₂ cup light corn syrup
¹/₂ cup shortening
¹/₃ cup brown sugar

BISCOTTINI ALL'UVETTA
Little Raisin Cookies
Makes about 3 dozen cookies

1. In a bowl, combine the flour and fruits.
2. In a saucepan, combine the corn syrup, shortening, and brown sugar and bring to a boil, stirring constantly. Remove from the heat and add the fruit mixture. Mix well.
3. Preheat the oven to 375°. Butter and flour 2 baking sheets. Drop the cookie batter by the teaspoon onto the baking sheets, placing them about 3 inches apart. Bake for 5 minutes, turn off the oven, and let the cookies stand inside for 5 minutes longer. Cool and serve.

PIZZELLE ALLA GUARDIESE
Pizzelle à la Guardiagrele
Makes about 60 *pizzelle*

Guardiagrele is a small town in Abruzzo perched on the top of a hill at the foot of the Maiella, second highest peak of the Apennine mountains. From a distance the town looks like a stone ship. At night, the ship becomes an enthroned queen wearing a crown of diamonds. I was born in Guardiagrele.

A *pizzelle* iron or machine is necessary for this recipe.

> 6 eggs
> 1¹/₂ cups sugar
> ¹/₂ pound (2 sticks) unsalted butter, melted and cooled
> 1 tablespoon vanilla extract
> 3¹/₂ cups all-purpose flour
> 1 tablespoon plus 1 teaspoon baking powder
> 1 cup finely chopped nuts (optional)

1. In a mixing bowl, beat the eggs, gradually adding the sugar. Still beating, add the butter, vanilla, and, a little at a time, the flour and the baking powder. Add the nuts, if desired. The mixture will have the consistency of a thick batter.
2. When the iron is heated, drop about 1 teaspoon of the batter in the center of the griddle and press down the lid. Cook for 30 seconds and remove. Let the *pizzelle* cool flat; serve in a basket.

NOTE: *Pizzelle* keep well in a tin box.

Parrozzo is a contraction of *pane rozzo* (rough bread), a rustic, sweetened bread that the shepherds of Abruzzo, in central Italy, ate for Christmas. A clever pastry maker from Pescara refined it into the now famous Parrozzo di Pescara. However, since the recipe is secret, this is my father's version.

PARROZZO DI PAPÀ
Papa's Rough Christmas Bread
Serves 10

6 eggs, separated
1¹/₂ cups sugar
1¹/₂ cups blanched almonds, toasted and ground very
** fine**
1 cup semolina
1 lemon
4 ounces semisweet chocolate
1 scant tablespoon unsalted butter
1 teaspoon freshly brewed espresso coffee (optional)
Chocolate shavings or curls

1. Preheat the oven to 375°. Butter a 9-inch dome-shaped casserole or ovenproof bowl. In a mixing bowl, beat the egg yolks and sugar until fluffy and lemon-colored. Add the almonds and semolina and mix. Grate the lemon peel into the mixture and squeeze in about 1 tablespoon of the lemon juice.

2. In another bowl, beat the egg whites until stiff. Fold into the egg yolk mixture. Pour into the prepared casserole and bake until a toothpick inserted in the center of the cake comes out clean, about 1 hour.

3. In a saucepan, melt together the chocolate and the butter, stirring constantly, over very low heat. Add the coffee, if desired. Spread the mixture over the cake, sprinkle with the chocolate shavings, and store in a cool place. This cake is always better when eaten a day or two after it is made.

NOTE: This *parrozzo* keeps well for a week or so. Wrap in foil or store in a tin box.

MACEDONIA DI FRUTTA
Fruit Mélange
Serves 6

This dessert is called Macedonia di Frutta because at the time of Alexander the Great, the country of Macedonia consisted of a melange of states. It is difficult to recommend precise quantities for this dessert or for the types of fruit—I like to use whatever is in season.

3 cups seasonal fruit such as apples, melons, peaches, or plums
2 tablespoons confectioners' sugar or honey (optional)
1/4 cup rum, kirschwasser, or Cognac
1/2 cup coarsely chopped walnuts (optional)
1/4 cup raisins (optional)
4 to 5 dried apricots (optional)

1. Dice all the fruit. Add the sugar and mix well. Add the rum and the nuts, raisins, and apricots if desired. Toss well and chill.
2. Serve in individual glasses or bowls, accompanied by cookies if desired.

MARGHERITA DI FRUTTA ALL'ITALIANA
Italian-Style Fruit Marguerite
Serves 6

I invented this dessert for Marguerite Stevens, a sunny and serene friend.

2 pints fresh strawberries
3 kiwi fruits
3 tablespoons Centerba or Cointreau liqueur
1 pint vanilla ice cream or lemon sherbet

1. Stem the strawberries and slice them.
2. Peel and thinly slice the kiwi fruits. Cut each slice in half.
3. Reserve 6 slices of strawberry for the garnish. Divide the strawberries among 6 decorative dishes, forming a mound in each dish. Surround the mounds with a circle of kiwi slices and sprinkle each dish of fruit with 1/2 tablespoon of the liqueur. Each dish, when presented, should look like a daisy. Chill.
4. Just before serving, add a scoop of ice cream and top with a reserved strawberry slice.

The mythological Ermione was a nymph of the woods. In this case, Ermione is my friend the cookbook author and teacher Hermie Kranzdorf. This recipe is an adaptation of one of hers.

CREMA DI FRUTTA ERMIONE
Fruit Cream Hermione
Serves 8

1 envelope unflavored gelatin
1 cup sour cream
$^{1}/_{2}$ cup sugar
$^{1}/_{2}$ teaspoon vanilla extract
$^{1}/_{4}$ cup berries
1 cup heavy cream
$2^{1}/_{2}$ to 3 cups diced fruits or berries (see NOTE)

1. In a small saucepan, sprinkle the gelatin over $^{1}/_{4}$ cup water and set aside for a few minutes to soften. Heat, stirring, until the gelatin is dissolved.

2. In a food processor or blender, combine the dissolved gelatin with the sour cream, sugar, vanilla, and the $^{1}/_{4}$ cup berries. Purée until well blended and turn into a large bowl.

3. In a bowl, whip the cream until soft peaks form. Stir one-third of the whipped cream into the purée to lighten it, then fold in the remaining cream.

4. Drain the diced fruits well and fold them into the cream. Pour the fruit cream into individual serving dishes, glasses, or a serving bowl and refrigerate for 2 to 3 hours, until firm. It will keep well for a day or two if covered tightly and refrigerated.

NOTE: You can use almost any fruit or combination of fruits for this dessert. Strawberries, blueberries, and raspberries are all excellent. Or try diced peaches, nectarines, or even apricots.

The fruit purée lends both color and flavor to the basic cream. Berries will give the prettiest color, but almost any fruit will do.

MELE ALL'ANTICA
Antique-Style Apples
Serves 8

2 tea bags
1 cup sugar
Pinch of cinnamon
Pinch of ginger
2 strips of lemon zest
4 pounds not too ripe Golden Delicious apples
1/2 cup jam or marmalade
2 tablespoons orange-flavored liqueur (optional)
4 lemon slices

1. In a saucepan, bring 5 cups of water to a boil and add the tea bags. Remove from the heat and let stand 5 minutes. Discard the tea bags and mix in the sugar, cinnamon, ginger, and lemon zest. Mix well and bring the liquid to a boil over high heat.

2. Quarter the apples and peel and core them. Cook the wedges in the boiling liquid until tender. With a slotted spoon, remove the apple wedges to a serving dish and set aside to cool.

3. In a saucepan, combine the jam and liqueur if used, or 2 tablespoons of the liquid in which the apples cooked. Bring to a simmer and cook, stirring, for 2 to 3 minutes. Pour the sauce over the apples.

4. Cut the lemon slices into little wedges and insert them among the apples in a decorative fashion. Cool completely and serve.

PESCHE AL LAMBRUSCO
Peaches with Lambrusco Wine
Serves 6

A simple and refreshing summer dessert. And an excellent way to utilize Lambrusco.

6 large ripe peaches
6 teaspoons sugar (optional)
1 bottle Lambrusco wine, well chilled

1. Peel the peaches if you wish. Stone and slice them, dividing the slices among 6 individual goblets. Sprinkle each serving with 1 teaspoon sugar, if desired.

2. Chill until serving time. Just before serving, fill the goblets with Lambrusco.

6 navel oranges
2 cups sugar
1 cup hot water
1 teaspoon cream of tartar
¼ cup amaretto liqueur
2 kiwi fruits

ARANCE E KIWI ALL'AMARETTO
Oranges and Kiwis with Amaretto
Serves 6

1. Remove the zest from 3 of the oranges without removing the white pith. Cut the zest into very thin strips.

2. In a saucepan, combine the sugar, hot water, and cream of tartar and stir well. Add the orange zest and bring to a boil. Reduce the heat to low and simmer for about 30 minutes. Remove from the heat, add the amaretto, and chill.

3. Peel all of the oranges. Slice them into rounds and remove all of the seeds. Arrange the slices on a serving dish. Peel and slice the kiwis, and insert at regular intervals among the oranges. Spoon the cooked zest and some of the syrup over. Serve, with the remaining syrup on the side.

NOTE: Any leftover syrup may be reused, if you like.

2 tablespoons unsalted butter
6 ripe pears, such as Bosc or Anjou
2 tablespoons sugar
¼ cup amaretto, apricot, or Triple Sec liqueur

PERE AL LIQUORE
Pears in Liqueur
Serves 6

1. Preheat the oven to 350°. Butter a large pie dish from which you can serve. Set aside.

2. Peel the pears, halve them, and remove the cores and stems. Drop the halves into a bowl of water to prevent discoloration.

3. Pat the pears dry and set them, cut side down, in the buttered pan. Sprinkle with the sugar and dot with the remaining butter. Bake for 35 to 40 minutes, until soft but not mushy.

4. Sprinkle the hot pears with the liqueur. Cool and serve.

NOTE: Plums or prune plums may be substituted for the pears.

PERE ALLA GABRIELLA
Pears Gabriella
Serves 6

Gabriella Pace, a dear friend, served this dessert at one of her dinner parties. I liked it so much, I asked her to share the recipe with me.

12 firm pears with stems attached
3 cups dry white wine
¹/₄ cup sugar
3 whole cloves
1 small cinnamon stick
4 ounces semisweet chocolate, grated or finely chopped
1 cup heavy cream, whipped
1 batch zabaglione made with 6 egg yolks (see page 188)
Julienne-cut orange zest (optional)

1. Peel the pears, leaving the stems attached, and stand them in a nonreactive casserole. Add the wine, sugar, cloves, and cinnamon. Bring to a boil over moderate heat and cook until a fork penetrates the fruit easily, 10 to 20 minutes. Set aside to cool.

2. Remove the pears to a serving bowl and reduce the liquid, if necessary, over moderate heat until it becomes the consistency of a syrup. Pour over the pears and sprinkle them with the chocolate; some will melt into the hot syrup.

3. Just before serving, fold the whipped cream into cooled zabaglione and spoon the mixture over the pears. Decorate with the orange zest, if desired.

PERE E FORMAGGIO
Pears and Cheese

There is an Italian proverb which says, *"Al cafon non far sapere quant'e' buon formaggio e pere"*—Do not let the peasant know how good cheese and pears are. Why? If he knows, he will never bring those things to market; he will eat them himself. It is indeed a delightful, simple Italian dessert which goes very well as a finale for any dinner but especially one of pasta. You need ripe pears and one or two good cheeses, one mild and one sharp. Serve with crusty Italian bread, pears cored and quartered at the last minute and arranged on a nice dish, and cheese on a board. Serve a good glass of Rosatello Ruffino, or a light red such as Valpolicella or Bardolino.

3 pints fresh strawberries
3 tablespoons honey or 1 tablespoon confectioners' sugar
1/2 cup liqueur, such as strawberry, orange, or Frangelico
1 cup heavy cream

FRAGOLE IN SPUMA ROSA
Strawberries in Pink Foam
Serves 6

1. Wash, hull, and dry the strawberries. Reserve 6 of the ripest ones. Slice the remaining strawberries and place them in a mixing bowl. Add the honey and the liqueur and mix well. Chill.
2. In a large bowl, whip the cream and refrigerate it.
3. In a food processor or blender, purée the reserved strawberries. Fold the purée into the whipped cream.
4. Turn the sliced strawberries into a serving bowl or into individual bowls. Top with the pink whipped cream and serve.

2 pints strawberries
Juice of 1/2 orange
1/4 cup orange-flavored liqueur
1 cup whole-milk ricotta cheese
2 to 3 tablespoons confectioners' sugar
1 teaspoon vanilla extract
Candied orange peel, cut into thin strips or chopped

CUORICINI ALLA CREMA
Little Hearts in Cream
Serves 6

1. Stem the strawberries and cut them into heart-shaped slices. Place in a mixing bowl, sprinkle with the orange juice and liqueur, and chill.
2. In a food processor, combine the ricotta, sugar, and vanilla. Process to a smooth cream and chill.
3. Just before serving, turn the strawberries into a serving bowl or individual bowls and pour the ricotta sauce over them. Garnish with the candied orange.

SUSINE ALLA CREMA
Plums with Custard
Serves 6 to 8

10 large plums
Juice of $1/2$ lemon
$1/4$ cup plus 1 tablespoon sugar
4 egg yolks
1 teaspoon vanilla extract
3 tablespoons all-purpose flour
1 cup milk
3 tablespoons brandy or rum

1. Pit the plums and slice very thinly. Place the slices in a mixing bowl and sprinkle with the lemon juice and 1 tablespoon of the sugar. Chill.
2. In a saucepan, beat the egg yolks and the remaining $1/4$ cup of sugar. Add the vanilla, flour, and milk, blending well after each addition. Cook over low heat until the custard starts to "puff." Let it puff only 2 or 3 times. Remove from the heat and add the liquor.
3. Divide the plums among individual glasses or place in a large glass bowl. Reserve 1 slice to decorate each serving. Pour the custard over the prunes and decorate each with the reserved slices. Chill until ready to serve.

TORTA DI MANDORLE
Almond Cake
Serves 6 to 8

1 cup shelled almonds
$1^{1}/3$ cups granulated sugar
8 egg whites
$1/4$ teaspoon cream of tartar
$1/4$ teaspoon baking powder
Grated zest of 1 orange or 1 lemon
6 tablespoons all-purpose flour

1. Preheat the oven to 350°. Butter and flour a 9-inch springform pan. In a food processor, combine the almonds and 1 tablespoon of the sugar. Process until the almonds are finely chopped. Set aside.
2. In a bowl, combine the egg whites, cream of tartar, and baking powder. Beat, adding the remaining $1^{1}/4$ cups sugar a little at

a time, until the mixture holds stiff peaks. Fold in the orange zest and the almond mixture. Sift in the flour and continue folding until the mixture is thoroughly blended.

3. Pour the mixture into the prepared pan and smooth the top. Bake for about 1 hour, until a toothpick inserted in the center of the cake comes out clean. Cool and unmold.

4. Cut the cake with a serrated knife to prevent crumbling.

½ pound (2 sticks) unsalted butter, at room temperature
2 cups granulated sugar
6 eggs, separated
1½ cups sifted all-purpose flour
2 teaspoons baking powder
Grated zest of 1 orange
¼ cup plus 2 tablespoons blackberry liqueur
2 tablespoons milk
⅛ teaspoon cream of tartar
Confectioners' sugar
1 pint blackberries

TORTA ALLE MORE
Blackberry Cake
Serves 6 to 8

---

1. Preheat the oven to 350°. Butter a 10-inch springform tube pan and set aside. In a mixing bowl, beat the butter until fluffy. One cup at a time, add the sugar. One at a time, add the egg yolks, blending well after each addition.

2. Combine the flour and baking powder and beat them into the butter mixture. Add the orange zest, ¼ cup liqueur, and milk. Mix well and set aside.

3. In a medium bowl, combine the cream of tartar and the egg whites. Whip until stiff but not dry. Gently but thoroughly, fold the whites into the egg batter. Pour the batter into the prepared pan.

4. Bake for 1 hour, until a skewer inserted in the center of the cake comes out clean. Cool on a rack and unmold onto a cake dish. Dust the cake with confectioners' sugar. Fill the hole of the cake with blackberries and sprinkle with remaining blackberry liqueur. Serve.

PIZZA DOLCE ALL'ARANCIA E CIOCCOLATA

Orange and Chocolate Cake

Serves 8 to 10

DOUGH

2 cups all-purpose flour
2 tablespoons granulated sugar
Grated zest of 1 orange
2/3 cup vegetable shortening
2 egg yolks
Juice of 1 orange

FILLING

3/4 cup granulated sugar
1/4 cup cornstarch
3/4 cup unsweetened cocoa powder
3 cups half & half or light cream
2 cups heavy cream
1 1/2 tablespoons confectioners' sugar
1 teaspoon vanilla extract
Pinch of cinnamon
Chocolate shavings (optional)

1. Make the dough: In a food processor or a mixing bowl, combine the flour, sugar, and orange zest. Cut in the shortening until the mixture resembles coarse meal. Mix in the egg yolks and enough orange juice to gather the dough into a ball. Add a little water if the dough seems dry. The dough should not be sticky; do not handle too much. Wrap the dough in plastic or foil and chill.
2. Preheat the oven to 375°. Divide the dough into 5 equal parts and roll each part into a 9-inch circle. Trim evenly all around, using a 9-inch pot lid. Place the rounds on ungreased baking sheets. (You may have to do this in batches if you do not have a large oven.) Pierce the rounds with a fork and bake until lightly browned, 10 to 15 minutes.
3. Make the filling: In a zabaglione or copper pot, combine the sugar, cornstarch, and cocoa. Gradually add the half & half, beating vigorously. Cook the custard over low heat until thickened. Remove from the heat and cool, stirring often to prevent a skin from forming on the top.
4. In a bowl, whip the heavy cream with 1 tablespoon of the confectioners' sugar and the vanilla. Combine half of the whipped cream with the chocolate custard.
5. Assemble the pizza: Place one circle of dough on a serving

platter and spread with an even layer of the custard. Cover with a second circle and continue layering, leaving the last circle of dough uncovered.

6. Spread the remaining whipped cream on the sides and top of the cake. If you do not have enough, leave the top uncovered. Combine the remaining 1/2 tablespoon confectioners' sugar with the cinnamon and sprinkle on the cake. Decorate, if desired, with chocolate shavings.

---

10 egg yolks
2/3 cup sugar
10 tablespoons unsalted butter
8 ounces semisweet chocolate, coarsely chopped
1 cup very finely chopped walnuts (about 1 1/4 cups shelled nuts)
8 egg whites
3/4 cup apricot jam
2/3 cup coarsely chopped walnuts

TORTA DI CIOCCOLATA ALLE NOCI
Walnut Chocolate Cake
Serves 6 to 8

1. Preheat the oven to 350°. Butter a 9-inch springform pan. In a mixing bowl, combine the egg yolks and sugar. Do not beat; stir just to dissolve the sugar.

2. Place the butter and the chocolate in the top of a double boiler over hot water. Stir the mixture over low heat until melted and smooth. Slowly pour the chocolate into the egg mixture and mix well. Reserve 1 cup of the egg-chocolate mixture and set aside. Fold the very finely chopped walnuts into the remaining egg-chocolate mixture.

3. In a bowl, whip the egg whites until stiff but not dry. Gently fold the whites into the egg-chocolate mixture and pour into the prepared pan. Bake for 50 to 60 minutes, until the center feels springy to the touch.

4. Set the pan on a rack and let cool for 30 minutes. Run a spatula around the edge of the pan and let the cake fall gently. Remove the sides of the pan and let the cake cool completely.

5. Slice the cake into 2 layers. Spread the jam over the bottom layer and top with the remaining layer.

6. Frost the cake with the reserved egg-chocolate mixture. Pat the coarsely chopped walnuts around the sides of the cake and refrigerate. This cake is better if chilled, since its texture is fudge-like.

CASSATA ALLA SULMONESE
Sulmona-Style Cassata
Serves 12

This cake is traditionally served at Christmas in the City of Sulmona, in Abruzzo, birthplace of the Latin poet Ovid.

8 ounces *torrone* (nougat)
8 ounces *croccante* (almond brittle)
4 ounces milk chocolate
1 pound (4 sticks) unsalted butter, at room temperature
1/2 cup plus 2 tablespoons confectioners' sugar
6 egg yolks
2 to 3 tablespoons unsweetened cocoa powder
Amaretto, Centerba, or Cointreau liqueur
2 batches of Pan di Spagna Luciana Amore (see page 187), baked together in a 10-inch cake pan
Candied cherries and citron, for decoration

1. One at a time, chop the *torrone*, *croccante*, and milk chocolate. Set aside in three separate bowls.
2. In a mixing bowl, beat the butter while adding the sugar. Add the egg yolks, one at a time, and beat until well incorporated and fluffy.
3. Divide the butter cream into three parts; one portion should be larger than the other two. Combine the *torrone* and chocolate with one of the equal parts and the *croccante* with the other. Mix the larger third part with the cocoa and amaretto.
4. Split the sponge cake into three equal layers. Place one layer on a serving plate, sprinkle with the liqueur, and spread with the *torrone*-chocolate cream. Top with another layer, sprinkle with liqueur, and spread with the *croccante* cream. Place the last layer on top, sprinkle with liqueur, and spread the top and sides with the cocoa cream. Decorate with candied cherries and citron and chill overnight. Let come to room temperature before serving.

NOTE: This cake keeps well for three days in the refrigerator.

Cassata is not always an ice cream, but a cake. It is a Sicilian specialty which at one time was traditionally made for Easter. The classic one is a rather large flat cake covered with green marzipan over which rests a white lamb, made with sugar. Since it has become popular all over Italy and at every season, cassata is now only encircled with marzipan, while the top remains white, with a lone cherry set in the middle. However, Sicilians have a homemade version, and this is it.

CASSATA CASALINGA ALLA SICILIANA
Homemade Sicilian Cassata
Serves 8 to 10

3 cups whole-milk ricotta cheese
1¹/₂ cups sugar
2 tablespoons chopped candied orange peel
2 ounces semisweet chocolate, coarsely chopped
¹/₄ cup unsweetened cocoa powder
1 Pan di Spagna Luciana Amore (sponge cake, see page 187)
6 tablespoons dark rum
1 tablespoon pine nuts (*pignoli*), coarsely chopped
Candied fruit, including 6 to 8 cherries, for decoration
2 ounces semisweet chocolate, shaved, for decoration

1. Strain the ricotta through a food mill or fine sieve into a large bowl. Add 1 cup of the sugar and mix well.
2. Place half of the sweetened ricotta in another bowl and add the candied orange peel and the chopped chocolate. Mix and set aside.
3. To the other bowl, add the cocoa and mix with the ricotta. Add the remaining ¹/₂ cup sugar and mix well; set aside.
4. With a serrated knife, slice the sponge cake horizontally into 3 equal layers.
5. Place the bottom layer on a serving dish and sprinkle 2 tablespoons of the rum over it. Spread half of the "white" ricotta over the top.
6. Place the middle cake layer over the bottom layer and sprinkle with 2 tablespoons of the rum. Spread half of the "brown" ricotta over it.
7. Top with the remaining cake layer and sprinkle with the re-

maining 2 tablespoons rum. Coat with an even layer of the remaining white ricotta.

8. Using a short spatula, decorate the sides of the cake with the remaining brown ricotta. Sprinkle the sides of the cake with the chopped nuts and decorate the top with the candied fruit and shaved chocolate. Chill, covered, for at least 3 hours or overnight. Tightly wrap leftover cassata in plastic or foil and refrigerate.

LE MAZURKE DI MARY
Mary's Mazurka Cookies

This is a recipe from the kitchen of Mary Towner, my good friend, pupil, and an excellent cooking teacher in her own right.

14 tablespoons (1 ³/₄ sticks) unsalted butter, at room temperature
³/₄ cup plus 2 teaspoons sugar
4 hard-cooked egg yolks, mashed
2 teaspoons vanilla extract
2 cups all-purpose flour
Pinch of salt
1 egg white
1 cup blanched almonds, slivered, or other type of nuts, chopped

1. Butter an 11-by-8-inch cookie sheet. In a mixing bowl, beat the butter until fluffy. Add the sugar and beat until well creamed. Add the egg yolks and the vanilla and mix well. Slowly add the flour and salt. Pour the mixture onto the prepared pan, and pat down with your hands to make an even layer. Chill for 1 hour.

2. Preheat the oven to 350°. Combine the egg white with 1 tablespoon of water. Brush the cookie dough with the egg wash and sprinkle the almonds on top. Gently press the nuts into the dough. Bake for 20 to 30 minutes, until a toothpick inserted in the center comes out clean. Cool slightly and cut with a pastry wheel into small squares.

Index

acciughe
  mozzarella in carrozza con, 88
  salsa d', 145–146
aglio e olio, 36
agnello, ragù di peperoni e, 144
albicocche, sorbetto di, al Vov, 199
amaretti
  semifreddo di ricotta ed, 184
  torta di, 194–195
ananas, sorbetto di mortelle e, 197
anchovy(ies), 27
  Mimi's little casserole, 76
  and mozzarella sandwiches, fried, 88
  sauce, whole-wheat pasta with, 145–146
antipasti, see appetizers
appetizers, 71–108
  antipasto à la Giulianova, 101
  avocado with tunafish, 94
  baked frittata, 91
  bread and salami, 72
  cauliflower florets and dip, 74
  cheese soufflé, 88–89

cheese-stuffed eggplant, 86–87
chicken livers Abruzzo, 106
creamed salt cod, 97
eggplant with sauce, 86
eggs with caviar, 89
fisherman's pie, 92–93
fish with olives and capers, 93
fried mozzarella and anchovy sandwiches, 88
fried vegetables Federico Spera, 74
the glutton, 79
green chicken, 105
ham-wrapped asparagus, 77
Italian antipasto, 71
Ligurian tapenade in a salad, 85
Ligurian tuna and olive spread, 83
marinated mushrooms, 81
marinated zucchini, 77
mariner's antipasto, 103
melt-in-the-mouth eggs, 90
Mimi's little casserole, 76

mozzarella antipasto with herbs, 87
mushroom toast, 82–83
mussels in green sauce, 100
my *crostini*, 79–80
Neapolitan-style peppers, 75
New Year's Eve *cotechino*, 107
octopus antipasto, 102
piquant fennel antipasto, 72
salmon mousse, 92
salt cod Vicenza-style, 97–98
Sardinian peppers, 76
scallops with pesto, 98
shrimps à la connoisseur, 99
Sicilian caponata with San Bernardo sauce, 84–85
skewered sausages, 106
spinach and artichoke flan, 80
stuffed mushrooms with capers, 81
stuffed mushrooms with ham and salami, 82
stuffed squid, 104
Taranto-style mussels, 99–100

tomatoes Adriatic, 72
tricolored *baccalà*, 96
tripe Florentine-style, 107–108
tuna salami, 94
tunnied veal, 95
zucchini and squash pie, 78
apple(s)
    antique-style, 206
    tart with *croccante*, 193
apricot sherbet with Vov, 199
arance
    e kiwi all'amaretto, 207
    pizza dolce all', e cioccolata,
      212–213
artichoke(s), 27
    crunchy salad, 180
    farmer's pasta, 144
    Italian antipasto, 71
    and spinach flan, 80
arugola
    cavatelli con l', 161
    insalata di, e indivia belga, 163
    insalata di rape rosse ed, 165
arugula
    and Belgian endive salad, 163
    little dumplings with, 161
    and red beet salad, 165
    tricolored salad, 175
asparagi
    al limone, 164
    al prosciutto cotto, 77
asparagus
    garden greens, 176
    ham-wrapped, 77
    with lemon, 164
    romantic butterflies, 126–127
Autumn menus, 57–61
avocado(s)
    capricious salad, 172–173
    snowy salad, 178
    with tunafish, 94

baccalà, 96–98
    mantecato, 97
    tricolore, 96
    alla vincentina, 97–98

bavette, 19, 118
bean salad, two-, 167
béchamel, 42
beef rolls Foggia-style, 141
beet(s), red
    and arugula salad, 165
    little winter salad, 178
    streaked salad, 180
    and string bean salad, 164
bigoli, 15, 145–146
birthday dinner dishes, 61
biscottini all'uvetta, 201
blackberry cake, 211
bocconotti all'abruzzese, 196
bolognese sauce, 38
bread
    crumbs, 27
    Papa's rough Christmas, 203
    salad, 177
    and salami, 72
broccoli
    garden greens, 176
    tomato and cucumber salad
      with Gorgonzola, 165
brodo, 33, 129, 130
broth, 33, 129, 130
bucatini, 19
budino, 189–190
    di cioccolata, 189
    di ricotta, 190

cabbage Turin-style, 172
caffè
    cremolata al, 195
    granita di, 199
cake, 210–216
    almond, 210–211
    blackberry, 211
    chocolate, 213
    decorating, 34
    homemade Sicilian cassata,
      215–216
    home-style *zuppa inglese*, 185–
      186
    orange and chocolate, 212–213
    sponge, Luciana Amore's, 187

Sulmona-style cassata, 214
cannelloni, 15, 148–151
    Anna Teresa's, 148–149
    with mushrooms, ham, and
      cheese, 150–151
    stuffing for, 149
cannelloni, 15, 148–151
    alla Anna Teresa, 148–149
    all'etrusca, 150–151
capelli d'angelo, 22
capellini, 22
capers, 28
    fish with olives and, 93
    stuffed mushrooms with, 81
capesante al pesto, 98
*capodanno, insalata della vigilia
    di*, 179
caponata, Sicilian, with San
    Bernardo sauce, 84–85
*caponata alla siciliana con salsa
    San Bernardo*, 84–85
cappelletti, 18, 22
capperi
    funghi ripieni ai, 81
    pesce alle olive e, 93
caprese, la, 169
carbonara, spaghetti alla, 109
carciofi, sformato di spinaci e, 80
*carrozza, mozzarella in, con
    acciughe*, 88
cassata
    casalinga alla siciliana, 215–216
    alla sulmonese, 214
casserole, Mimi's little, 76
cauliflower
    florets and dip, 74
    garden greens, 176
    New Year's Eve salad, 179
    salad, 167
    white or purple, pasta with,
      133
cavatelli, 15, 161
caviale, uova al, 89
caviar, eggs with, 89
cavolfiore
    antipasto di, 74

bianco o nero, pasta col, 133
   insalata di, 167
cavoli, insalata di, alla torinese,
   172
cetrioli
   insalata di, al Gorgonzola, 165
   insalata di pomodori e, 169
cheese(s)
   antipasto, 86–89
   beef rolls Foggia-style, 141
   cannelloni with mushrooms,
      ham and, 150–151
   four, macaroni with, 132
   four, noodles with, 122
   lasagna, *see* lasagna
   Mimi's little casserole, 76
   Nordic macaroni, 137
   and pears, 208
   smoked pasta, 134
   soufflé, 88–89
   spaghetti tossed with bacon,
      butter, eggs and, 109
   stuffed eggplant, 86–87
   tricolored salad, 175
   types of, 31–32
   *see also specific cheeses and
      pasta recipes*
chicche verdi, 16, 160
chicken
   broth, 130
   green, 105
chicken livers Abruzzo, 106
chocolate, 28, 212–213
   cake, 213
   and orange cake, 212–213
   pudding, 189
Christmas bread, Papa's rough,
   203
Christmas dishes, 66
ciambotta alla Federico Spera,
   74
cioccolata, 28, 212–213
   budino di, 189
   pizza dolce all'arancia e, 212–
      213
   torta di, alle noci, 213

cod, salt, 96–98
   creamed, 97
   tricolored, 96
   Vicenza style, 97–98
coffee
   ice, 199
   pudding, 195
cookies, little raisin, 201
*cotechino della vigilia di
   capodanno*, 107
cozze, 99–100
   con la salsa verde, 100
   spaghetti con le, alla napoletana,
      119
   alla tarantina, 99–100
cranberry and pineapple sherbet,
   197
crema
   di Mamma, 188
   susine alla, 210
cremolata al caffe, 195
croccante, crostata di mele al,
   193
crostata, 191–194
   di crema Jolanda, 191
   di mele al croccante, 193
   di pesche con ricotta, 192
   pasta per, 194
crostini miei, 79–80
crostoni ai funghi, 82–83
cucumber
   broccoli and tomato salad with
      Gorgonzola, 165
   streaked salad, 180
   and tomato salad, 169
cuoricini alla crema, 209
custard
   Mama's, 188
   plums with, 210

desserts, 183–216
   almond cake, 210–211
   amaretti torte, 194–195
   antique-style apples, 206
   apple tart with *croccante*, 193
   apricot sherbet with Vov, 199

blackberry cake, 211
Carmelina's ice cream truffle,
   200
champagne sherbet, 198
chocolate pudding, 189
classic zabaglione, 188
coffee ice, 199
coffee pudding, 195
cold peach soufflé with rum,
   186
cranberry and pineapple
   sherbet, 197
drowned samoca, 201
fruit cream Hermione, 205
fruit mélange, 204
golden froth, 189
homemade Sicilian cassata,
   215–216
home-style *zuppa inglese*, 186–
   187
Italian-style fruit Marguerite,
   204
Jolanda's cream pie, 191
lemon mousse, 183–184
little hearts in cream, 209
little raisin cookies, 201
little stuffed pies, 196
Luciana Amore's sponge cake,
   187
Mama's custard, 188
orange and chocolate cake,
   212–213
oranges and kiwis with
   Amaretto, 207
Papa's rough Christmas bread,
   203
peach and ricotta pie, 192–193
peaches with Lambrusco wine,
   206
pears and cheese, 208
pears Gabriella, 208
pears in liqueur, 207
pizzelle à la Guardiagrele, 202
plums with custard, 210
ricotta and *amaretti* mousse,
   184

ricotta pudding, 190
strawberries in pink foam, 209
strawberry mousse, 185
Sulmona-style cassata, 214
tart dough, 194
walnut chocolate cake, 213
dolci, see desserts
dough, pasta, 7–14
    cooking, 13
    cutting, by hand, 10
    cutting, by hand-operated
        machine, 12
    making, by hand, 8
    making, in food processor, 8–9
    rolling, by hand, 9
    rolling, by hand-operated
        machine, 11
dough, tart, 194
dumplings, 160–161
    Grandpa's green, 160
    little, with arugula, 161

Easter dishes, 51
eggplant(s)
    Bari-style, 166
    cheese-stuffed, 86–87
    Mediterranean, 168
    with sauce, 86
    Siracusa-style salad, 170–171
egg(s)
    with caviar, 89
    melt-in-the-mouth, 90
    whites, freezing, 34
fagioli, insalata di due, 167
fagiolini
    insalata rosata di, 164
    insalata semplice di, 169
    mimosa, insalata di, 168
farfalle, 20, 126–127
    dell'estate, 131–132
    romantiche, 126–127
    con la salsa cruda, 126
fegatini all'abruzzese, antipasto di,
    106

*fegato d'oca, tortellini con la salsa
    di,* 154–155
fennel antipasto, piquant, 73
fettuccine, 16, 18, 22
finocchi in pinzimonio, 73
fish
    antipasto à la Guilianova, 101
    mariner's antipasto, 103
    with olives and capers, 93
    pie, 92–93
    tomatoes Adriatic, 72
flan, spinach and artichoke, 80
forchettone, 26
forks, wooden, 26
formaggio, 86–89
    melanzane ripiene al, 86–87
    pere e, 208
    quattro, maccheroni ai, 132
    quattro, tagliolini ai, 122
    sufflé al, 88–89
fragole
    semifreddo di, 185
    in spuma rosa, 209
freselle, 177
frittata, 34, 91
fruit, 204–205
    cream Hermione, 205
    Marguerite, Italian-style, 204
    mélange, 204
    see also specific fruits
frutta, 204–205
    crema di, Ermione, 205
    Macedonia di, 204
    Margherita di, all'italiana, 204
funghi, 29, 81–83
    crostoni ai, 82–83
    *farciti al prosciutto cotto e
        salame,* 82
    maccheroni alla chitarra coi,
        136–137
    marinati, 81
    ripieni ai capperi, 81
fusilli, 20
    farmer's, 144–145
    Franca Falcone's, 136

with lamb and pepper ragout
    Abruzzo-style, 144
    smoked, 134
    summer, 131
fusilli, 20
    affumicata, 134
    dell'estate, 131–132
    del fattore, 144–145
    alla Franca Falcone, 136
    *con ragù d'agnello e peperoni
        all'abruzzese,* 144

ghiotta, la, 79
giardiniera, 176
glossary, pasta, 15–22
gnocchi, 16, 157–160
    Giordano-style, 157
    green, Grandpa's, 160
    Roman-style semolina, 159
    tricolored potato, 158
gnocchi, 16, 157–160
    alla giordano, 157
    di patate tricolore, 158
    di semolina, 16, 159
    verdi, 16, 160
goose liver sauce, tortellini in,
    154–155
Gorgonzola, broccoli, tomato,
    and cucumber salad with,
    165
*Gorgonzola, insalata di broccoli,
    pomodori, e cetrioli al,* 165
granita di caffè, 199

ham, *see* prosciutto
handmade dough, 8, 9, 10
hand-operated machine, rolling
    and cutting dough with, 11–
    12
homemade pasta, 7–18

ice, coffee, 199
ice cream truffle, Carmelina's,
    200
ingredients, 27–32

insalata, 163–181
  di arugola e indivia belga, 163
  asparagi al limone, 164
  di broccoli, pomodori, e cetrioli
    al Gorgonzola, 165
  di calpurnia, 173
  la caprese, 169
  capricciosa, 172–173
  di cavolfiori, 167
  di cavoli alla torinese, 172
  colorata, 175
  croccante, 180
  di du fagioli, 167
  di fagiolini mimosa, 168
  genovese, 171
  giardiniera, 176
  giornaliera, 181
  invernale, 178
  melanzane alla barese, 166
  melanzane mediterranee, 168
  alla neve, 178
  panzanella della casa, 177
  peperoni arrostiti, 177
  di pomodori e cetrioli, 169
  di rape rosse ed arugola, 165
  rosata di fagiolini, 164
  russa, 174
  semplice di fagiolini, 169
  alla siciliana, 172
  alla siracusana, 170–171
  tapenata ligure in, 85
  di tonno Mamma e Papà, 176
  tricolore, 175
  variegata, 180
  della vigilia di capodanno, 179
  di zucchine, 170
invernale, insalatina, 178
involtini alla foggiana, 141
lamb and pepper ragout, pasta
  with, Abruzzo-style, 144
Lambrusco wine, peaches with, 206
lasagna, 16, 21, 127–129
  in broth Lanciano-style, 129
  curly, timbale with salmon, 127
  green, Modena-style, 128

lasagne, 16, 21, 127–129
  in brodo alla lancianese, 129
  ricce, 21, 127
  verdi, 16, 128
lemon
  asparagus with, 164
  mousse, 183–184
lettuce, *see* salads
limone
  asparagi al, 164
  spuma di, 183–184
linguine, 19, 120–121
  fisherman's, 121
  with mussels Neapolitan style,
    119
  peasant style, 110
  with pesto, 114
  with squid sauce, 120
linguine, 19, 120–121
  alla contadina, 110
  con le cozze alla napoletana, 119
  al pesto, 114
  del pescatore, 121
  al sugo di seppie, 120

macaroni, 17, 130–139, 142–145
  angry, 138
  bully's, 139
  in earthenware, 135
  farmer's, 144–145
  with four cheeses, 132
  Franca Falcone's, 136
  with green and red sauce Lella,
    130–131
  guitar, with mushrooms, 136–
    137
  with lamb and pepper ragout
    Abruzzo style, 144
  Nordic, 137
  Sardinian, 134
  smoked, 134
  summer, 131–132
  timbale, Grandmother's, 142–
    143
  with white or purple

cauliflower, 133
maccheroni, 17, 130–139, 142–145
  affumicata, 134
  all'arrabbiata, 138
  alla burina, 139
  col cavolfiore bianco o nero, 133
  alla chitarra, 17, 136–137
  al coccio, 135
  dell'estate, 131–132
  del fattore, 144–145
  alla Franca Falcone, 136
  alla nordica, 137
  ai quattro formaggi, 132
  con ragù d'agnello e peperoni
    all'abruzzese, 144
  alla sarda, 134
  col sughetto acerbo alla Lella,
    130–131
  timballo di, alla Nonnina, 142–
    143
Macedonia di frutta, 204
maltagliati, 16
marinara sauce, 37
mayonnaise, 41
meat
  Italian antipasto, 71
  sauce, 39
  sauce for pasta, 40
  see also specific meats
meat balls, tiny, 143
Mediterranean cuisine, 13
mélange, fruit, 204
melanzane, 86–87
  alla barese, 166
  mediterranee, 168
  in potacchio, 86
  ripiene al formaggio, 86–87
mele
  all'antica, 206
  crostata di, al croccante, 193
menus, 43–67
  Autumn, 57–61
  Spring, 47–51
  Summer, 52–56
  Winter, 62–67

more, torta alle, 211
mortelle, sorbetto di, e ananas, 197
mousse, 183–185
  lemon, 183–184
  ricotta and *amaretti,* 184
  salmon, 92
  strawberry, 185
mozzarella, 31, 87–88
  and anchovy sandwiches, fried, 88
  antipasto with herbs, 87
mozzarella, 87–88
  in carrozza con acciughe, 88
  all'erbette, antipasto di, 87
mushroom(s), 29, 79–83
  cannelloni with ham, cheese and, 150–151
  guitar macaroni with, 136–137
  marinated, 81
  my *crostini,* 79–80
  stuffed, with capers, 81
  stuffed, with ham and salami, 82
  toast, 82–83
mussels, 33, 99–100
  in green sauce, 100
  Neapolitan-style, spaghetti with, 119
  Taranto-style, 99–100

New Year's Eve *cotechino,* 107
New Year's Eve salad, 179
New Year's Eve supper dishes, 67
noodles, 119–125
  Capri-style egg, with vegetables and vodka, 124
  with four cheeses, 122
  green, with salmon, 123
  with lemon, 122–123
  straw and hay à la Anna Teresa, 119–120
  thick square, Daunia-style, 140
  timbale, financier-style, 125

oca', tortellini con la salsa di fegato d', 154–155
octopus antipasto, 102

orange(s)
  and chocolate cake, 212–213
  and kiwis with Amaretto, 207
  Sicilian-style salad, 172
orzo, 20, 156

paglia e fieno alla Anna Teresa, 119–120
pan di spagna Luciana Amore, 187
pane e salame, 72
panzanella della casa, 177
pappardelle, 17
parrozzo di papa, 203
pasta
  appetizers before, 71–108
  in Autumn, 57–61
  basic information about, 1–42
  basic sauces for, 35–42
  commercial, 19–22
  commercial egg, 22
  cooking, 13
  desserts after, 183–216
  draining, 34
  glossary of, 15–22
  helpful hints about, 33–34
  homemade, 7–14, 15–18
  and ingredients, 27–32
  leftover cooked, 14, 34
  long, 19
  menus, 43–67
  recipes, 69–216
  salads with, 163–181
  short, 20
  special cut, 21
  in Spring, 47–51
  in Summer, 52–56
  tools and utensils for, 23–26
  in Winter, 62–67
pasta corta, 20
pasta dishes, 109–161
  Genoa-style vegetable soup, 156
  romantic butterflies, 126–127
  with uncooked sauce, 126
  whole-wheat, with anchovy sauce, 145–146
  see also specific pastas

pasta lunga, 19
pasticcio
  di lasagne ricce al salmone, 127
  di tagliatelle alla finanziera, 125
patate tricolore, gnocchi di, 158
peach(es)
  with Lambrusco wine, 206
  and ricotta pie, 192–193
  soufflé with rum, cold, 186
pears, 207–208
  and cheese, 208
  Gabriella, 208
  in liqueur, 207
peasant's sauce, 41
penne, 20
  affumicata, 134
  all'arrabbiata, 138
  col cavolfiore bianco o nero, 133
  al coccio, 135
  del fattore, 144–145
  ai quattro formaggi, 132
  alla sarda, 134
  col sughetto acerbo alla Lella, 130–131
peperoni
  arrostiti, 177
  alla napoletana, 75
  ragù d'agnello e, 144
  alla sarda, 76
peppers, bell, 30
  capricious salad, 172–173
  the glutton, 79
  and lamb ragout, pasta with, Abruzzo-style, 144
  little winter salad, 178
  Mimi's little casserole, 76
  Neapolitan-style, 75
  roasted, 33, 177
  Sardinian, 76
  Siracusa-style salad, 170–171
peppers, hot, 30
perciatelli, 19
  al pesto, 114
  con le sarde alla palermitana, 118
pere, 207–208

e formaggio, 208
   alla Gabriella, 208
   al liquore, 207
pesce, alle olive e capperi, 93
pesche
   crostata di ricotta con, 192–193
   al Lambrusco, 206
   spuma di rum al, 186
pesto, 98, 114
pesto sauce, 98, 114
picnic dishes, 56
pies, appetizer
   fisherman's, 92–93
   zucchini and squash, 78
pies, dessert
   Jolanda's cream, 191
   little stuffed, 196
   peach and ricotta, 192–193
pineapple and cranberry sherbet, 197
pizza dolce all'arancia e cioccolata, 212–213
pizzelle alla guardiese, 202
plums with custard, 210
pollo
   brodo di, 130
   al verde, 105
polpi, antipasto di, 102
pomodori, 30
   all'adriatica, 72
   insalata di, 165
   insalata di cetrioli e, 169
porcini, 29, 79–80, 136–137
potacchio, melanzane in, 86
potato(es)
   Genoa-style salad, 171
   the glutton, 79
   gnocchi, tricolored, 158
   gnocchi Giordano-style, 157
   Grandpa's green dumplings, 160
prosciutto, 29–30, 33
   Amatrice-style pasta, 117
   cannelloni with mushrooms, cheese and, 150–151
   pasta in earthenware, 135

romantic butterflies, 126–127
   stuffed mushrooms with salami and, 82
   wrapped asparagus, 77
prosciutto, 29–30, 33
   cotto, asparagi al, 77
   cotto, funghi farciti al salame e, 82
pudding
   chocolate, 189
   coffee, 195
   ricotta, 190

quadrucci, 18

ragout
   lamb and pepper, pasta with, Abruzzo style, 144
   meat, for pasta, 40
ragù
   d'agnello e peperoni all'abruzzese, pasta con, 144
   all'italiana, 40
rape rosse ed arugola, insalata di, 165
ravioli, 18, 22
   ricotta-stuffed, 150
   stuffing for, 149
ravioli, 18, 22
   di ricotta, 149, 150
recipes, 69–216
   appetizers, 71–108
   desserts, 183–216
   for homemade pasta, 7–14
   pasta, 109–161
   salads, 163–181
ricotta, 32
   and *amaretti* mousse, 184
   and peach pie, 192–193
   pudding, 190
   stuffed ravioli, 150
ricotta
   budino di, 190
   crostata di pesche con, 192–193
   ravioli di, 150
   semifreddo di, ed amaretti, 184

rigati
   ai quattro formaggi, 132
   alla sarda, 134
rigatoni, 20, 21
   bully's, 139
   farmer's, 144–145
   with green and red sauce Lella, 130–131
   with lamb and pepper ragout Abruzzo-style, 144
   Sardinian, 134
   smoked, 134
   with white or purple cauliflower, 133
rigatoni, 20, 21
   affumicata, 134
   alla burina, 139
   col cavolfiore bianco o nero, 133
   del fattore, 144–145
   con ragù d'agnello e peperoni all'abruzzese, 144
   alla sarda, 134
   col sughetto acerbo alla Lella, 130–131
rotelle, 20, 21
   dell'estate, 131–132
   con la salsa cruda, 126
Russian salad, 174

salads, 163–181
   arugula and Belgian endive, 163
   asparagus with lemon, 164
   Bari-style eggplant, 166
   beet and string bean, 164
   bread, 177
   broccoli, tomato, and cucumber with Gorgonzola, 165
   Calpurnia's, 173
   capricious, 172–173
   Capri-style, 169
   cauliflower, 167
   colorful, 175
   crunchy, 180
   everyday, 181

garden greens, 176
Genoa-style, 171
Ligurian tapenade in, 85
little winter, 178
Mediterranean eggplant, 168
mimosa, string bean, 168
Mother and Father's tuna, 176
New Year's Eve, 179
red beet and arugula, 165
roasted peppers, 177
Russian, 174
Sicilian-style, 172
simple string bean, 169
Siracusa-style, 170–171
snowy, 178
streaked, 180
tomato and cucumber, 169
tricolored, 175
Turin-style cabbage, 172
two-bean, 167
zucchini, 170
salame
 *funghi farciti al prosciutto cotto
  e,* 82
 pane e, 72
 di tonno, 94
salami
 and bread, 72
 stuffed mushrooms with ham
  and, 82
 tuna, 94
salmon
 curly lasagne timbale with, 127
 green noodles with, 123
 mousse, 92
salmone
 pasticcio di lasagne ricce al, 127
 spuma al, 92
 tagliatelle verdi al, 123
salsa, see sauces
salsicce allo spiedo, 106
samoca, drowned, 201
samoca affogato, 201
sandwiches, fried mozzarella and
  anchovy, 88
sarde, pasta con le, alla

palermitana, 118
sardines, Palermo-style pasta
  with, 118
sauces
 anchovy, 145–146
 basic, 35–42
 béchamel, 42
 bolognese, 38
 eggplant with, 86
 garlic and oil, 36
 goose liver, 154–155
 green, 100
 harlots', 115
 Lella, green and red, 130–131
 marinara, 37
 mayonnaise, 41
 meat, 39
 meat, for pasta, 40
 Mediterranean cuisine and, 13
 my, 37
 peasant's, 41
 pesto, 114
 San Bernardo, 84
 squid, 120
 tomato, 36
 uncooked, 126
 zabaglione, 188
sausages, 106–107
 New Year's Eve, 107
 skewered, 106
scallops with pesto, 98
scampi alla buongustaia, 99
semifreddo, 184–185
 di fragole, 185
 di ricotta ed amaretti, 184
semolina, 30, 159
*seppie, linguine o spaghetti al sugo
  di,* 120
sformato di spinaci e carciofi, 80
shellfish
 antipasto à la Guilianova, 101
 Calpurnia's salad, 173
 fisherman's linguine, 121
 mariner's antipasto, 103
 see also specific shellfish
sherbet, 197–199

apricot, with Vov, 199
 champagne, 198
 cranberry and pineapple, 197
shrimp(s)
 à la connoisseur, 99
 tomatoes Adriatic, 72
sorbetto, 197–199
 allo spumante, 198
 di albicocche al Vov, 199
 di mortelle e ananas, 197
soufflé
 cheese, 88–89
 cold peach, with rum, 186
soup, Genoa-style vegetable, 156
spaghetti, 19, 109–120
 Amatrice-style, 177
 fisherman's, 121
 Lia Saraceni's, with harlots'
  sauce, 115
 with mussels Neapolitan-style,
  119
 Nerano-style, 116
 Palermo-style, with sardines,
  118
 peasant-style, 110
 with pesto, 114
 poultry man's, 111
 springtime, 112–113
 with squid sauce, 120
 tossed with bacon, butter, eggs,
  and cheese, 109
spaghetti, 19, 109–120
 all'amatriciana, 117
 alla carbonara, 109
 alla contadina, 110
 con le cozze alla napoletana, 119
 con le sarde alla palermitana,
  118
 alla nerano, 116
 del pescatore, 121
 al pesto, 114
 del pollaiolo, 11
 primavera, 112–113
 alla puttanesca Lia Saraceni,
  115
 al sugo di seppie, 120

spinach and artichoke flan, 80
spinaci, sformato di carciofi e, 80
spoons, wooden, 26
Spring menus, 47–51
spuma
  al salmone, 92
  di limone, 183–184
  di pesche al rum, 186
  rosa, fragole in, 209
spumante, sorbetto allo, 198
spumone all'aurum, 189
squash and zucchini pie, 78
squid
  sauce, linguine or spaghetti
    with, 120
  stuffed, 104
strawberry(ies)
  little hearts in cream, 209
  mousse, 186
  in pink foam, 209
string bean(s)
  and beet salad, 164
  garden greens, 176
  Genoa-style salad, 171
  salad, simple, 169
  salad mimosa, 168
sufflé al formaggio, 88–89
sugo, see sauces
Summer menus, 52–56
susine alla crema, 210

tagliatelle, 16, 18, 22, 122–125
  alla caprese, 124
  al limone, 122–123
  pasticcio di, alla finanziera, 125
tagliatelle verdi, 16, 18, 123
taglierini, 18
tagliolini, 18, 122
tapenade, Ligurian, 83
  in a salad, 85
tapenata alla ligure, 83
  in insalata, 85
tart
  apple, with *croccante,* 193
  dough, 194
tartufo di Carmelina, il, 200

tegamino alla Mimi, 76
timbale, 34
  curly lasagne, with salmon, 127
  financier-style *tagliatelle,* 125
  Grandmother's macaroni, 142–143
  standing ziti, 146–147
timballo, 34
  di maccheroni alla Nonnina, 142–143
  di zitoni all'impiedi, 146–147
tomato(es), 30, 33
  Adriatic, 72
  broccoli and cucumber salad
    with Gorgonzola, 165
  Capri-style salad, 169
  and cucumber salad, 169
  New Year's Eve salad, 179
  sauce, 36
  tricolored salad, 175
tonno, 31, 94–95
  avocado al, 94
  insalata di, Mamma e Papà, 176
  salame di, 94
  vitello, 95
tools, 23–26
torta
  di amaretti, 194–195
  di cioccolata alle noci, 213
  di mandorle, 210
  alle more, 211
  del pescatore, 92–93
torte, amaretti, 194–195
tortellini, 18, 22, 152–155
  in goose liver sauce, 154–155
  summer, 152–153
  truffled, with cream, 153–154
tortellini, 18, 22, 152–155
  dell'estate, 152–153
  con la salsa di fegato d'oca, 154–155
  tartuffati alla panna, 153–154
tortino fantasia, 91
totani ripieni, 104
trenette, 19, 114
tripe Florentine style, 107–108

trippa alla fiorentina, 107–108
troccoli, 18, 140
truffle, Carmelina's ice cream, 200
truffles, 31, 153–154
tubetti, 20, 156
tuna, 31, 94–95
  avocado with, 94
  Franca Falcone's fusilli, 136
  and olive spread, Ligurian, 83
  salad, Mother and Father's, 176
  salami, 94
tunnied veal, 95

utensils, 23–26
uova, 89–90
  al caviale, 89
  delicate, 90

veal, tunnied, 95
vegetables, 33
  Capri-style egg noodles with
    vodka and, 124
  Federico Spera, fried, 74
  soup, Genoa-style, 156
  see also salads; *specific vegetables*
verdure, zuppa di, alla genovese, 156
vitello tonnato, 95
Vov, apricot sherbet with, 199

whole-wheat pasta, 7, 145–146
wine, 32
Winter menus, 62–67

zabaglione, classic, 188
zabaglione classico, 188
ziti, 20, 21
  with four cheeses, 132
  with green and red sauce Lella, 130–131
  timbale, standing, 146–147
  with white or purple
    cauliflower, 133
ziti, 20, 21

col cavolfiore bianco o nero, 133
ai quattro formaggi, 132
col sughetto acerbo alla Lella,
    130–131
  timballo di, all'impiedi, 146–147
zitoni, 20, 146–147
zucchine

alla hodgypodgy, 78
insalata di, 170
a scapece, 77
zucchini, 77–79
  the glutton, 79
  marinated, 77
  Nerano-style pasta, 116

salad, 170
Sardinian pasta, 134
and squash pie, 78
zuppa di verdure alla genovese, 156
zuppa inglese casa mia, 186–187